WALKING IN CYPRUS

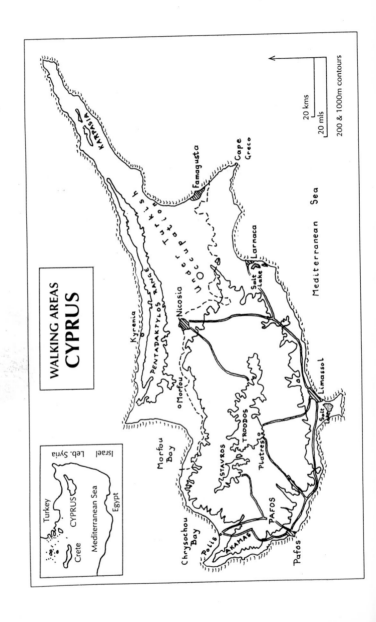

WALKING AREAS
CYPRUS

Turkey
CYPRUS
Crete
Mediterranean Sea
Leb. Syria
Israel
Egypt

KARPASIA

Famagusta
Cape Greco

Kyrenia
PENTADAKTYLOS RANGE

Troodos

Nicosia

Larnaca
Salt Lake

Mediterranean Sea

Morfou
oMorfou

Morfou Bay

Salt Lake
Limassol

STAVROS
TROODOS
Platrésio

Chrysochou Bay
Polis

AKAMAS
PAFOS

Pafos

20 kms
20 mls
200 & 1000m contours

WALKING IN CYPRUS

by

DONALD BROWN

CICERONE PRESS
MILNTHORPE, CUMBRIA

Acknowledgements

The author owes much to the friendly co-operation, practical walking experience and local knowledge of Philios Phylaktis, Director of Anthology Travels in Nicosia. He is also very grateful to Waymark and Ramblers Holidays for the experience gained while leading their walking groups on the island. Warm thanks go the Cyprus Tourism Office in Nicosia and the Cyprus High Commission in London for full and specific responses to requests for information.

Front Cover: Ascent to the Anogia plateau on the way from Pano Arodes to Cape Drepanon

CONTENTS

Route grading: the more stars, the more demanding the walk

AKAMAS ROUTES

PAFOS ROUTES

STAVROS FOREST ROUTE

MOUNT OLYMPUS ROUTES

OTHER TROODOS ROUTES

Advice to Readers

Readers are advised that whilst every effort is taken by the author to ensure the accuracy of this guidebook, changes can occur which may affect the contents. A book of this nature with specific descriptions is more prone to change than others. Waymarking alters, there may be new buildings or eradication of old buildings. It is advisable to check locally on transport, accommodation, shops etc but even rights-of-way can be altered and, more especially overseas, paths can be eradicated by landslip, forest fires or changes of ownership. The publisher would welcome notes of any such changes for future editions.

Asphodel

INTRODUCTION

SIZE AND LOCATION

Third largest island in the Mediterranean, Cyprus lies at the east end of the sea, in the angle between Turkey and Syria. It stretches 225kms/140mls from west to east, of which 74kms/46mls are the slender north-eastern peninsula. The greatest north-south dimension is 96kms/60mls. Its coastline measures 782kms/486mls. The whole area, 9251sq kms/3572sq mls, equals Norfolk and Suffolk combined. The Turks currently occupy just over a third, 3422sq kms/1322sq mls, about the same as Suffolk.

LANDSCAPE

For Cyprus, creation began twenty million years ago, when molten rock erupted from the sea floor, forming a mountainous island. On its northern side, another island surfaced and sank three times.

Between them, the sea bed rose to become the sedimentary Mesaoria Plain, stretching across Cyprus from Morfou Bay to Famagusta Bay. Its largely low-lying alluvium is fertile but treeless, crossed by seasonal rivers.

The original northern island has become the Kyrenia or Pentadaktylos range. Never more than 5kms/3mls wide, this forms a 1000m/3300ft high ridge of fissured limestone ravines, running west-east for 80kms/50mls along the north coast of Cyprus. Prevailing winds affect the north-facing slope, making it wetter and cooler, with a richer flora, than the southern side.

The southern island is now the Troodos range covering 3200sq kms/1235sq mls. It stretches from Stavrovouni in the east to Panagia in the west. Weather-resistant igneous rocks shape its tops as domes rather than spires. The range has no cliffs or gorges, unlike the craggier north.

Its major peaks rise steeply out of thick forests, six topping 1300m/4300ft. The mountains precipitate enough rain (up to 1000mm/38ins p.a.) to feed the half-dozen rivers that fill the country's reservoirs.

Troodos attracts international geological interest. On Mount Olympus, rocks and mineral crystals, formed as part of the ancient oceanic crust, are evident. Around the central mass rise foothills of pillow lava, formed by fast cooling after the original eruption.

Ancient copper deposits may have given Cyprus its name from the Greek *kypros*. Slag heaps date copper extraction to 2700 BC. The island was also an ancient source of asbestos, with the open-cast mine at Pano Amiandos producing up to 40,000 tons annually.

Over to the west, sedimentary as well as metamorphic rocks form the Pafos region.

Peninsulas, bays and headlands shape the coastline. Akamas is like a rhino's horn in the west; Karpasia is the north-eastern tail. Salt lakes perforate the south coast at Larnaca and Limassol.

NATURAL HISTORY

In this one small island, natural habitats range from sub-alpine, through garrigue, forest and maquis to semi-desert and Mediterranean coastal. 1800 plant species flower there, with 50 varieties of butterfly, 23 reptile and 16 mammal types.

THE SEA

250 species of fish swim the seas of Cyprus. The waters are clear, minimally polluted and rich with colourful life. Bathers often share the water with silvery two-banded bream. Green and loggerhead turtles breed on the warm beaches west and north of the Akamas peninsula. There are urchins, starfish and anemones. Even the sea shells are brightly coloured.

FARMING

The island's major crops are grapes, potatoes, oranges, barley, grapefruit, lemons, wheat. Flocks of sheep and goats are controlled to protect the land. Goat milk and cheese are sold. A few camels remain in the Turkish-held sector. Locusts were once a pest, devastating crops and causing famine.

PLANTS

While much of the flora of Cyprus has developed endemically in its insular isolation, many species have still arrived from neighbouring land-masses.

On Mount Olympus, the local interaction of geology, altitude, rainfall and temperature creates unusual conditions. Of 130 plants endemic to Cyprus, nearly half can be found within a few kilometres of the peak. Some indigenous types can be found only there.

Alyssum troodi likes the north-facing flanks of Olympus. Its yellow flowers shine on the bare rocks in May and June. The plant was used as a herbal remedy for rabies. Wild thyme made a herbal disinfectant and a medicine against diarrhoea.

Long seed-pods hang from *Arabis purpurea* on shaded rock above 700m/2300ft. Their Greek name *Dakrya tis Panayias* calls them the Virgin Mary's Tears. From February to April, the Cyprus crocus pushes its white and lilac flowers through the melting snow. Peonies follow with their pink flowers on red stems.

Troodos orchids are common in June under the forest shade above 300m/1000ft. March is the best month for lowland orchids, although many types can be found in flower at other times.

Yellow flowers of a dense dwarf broom carpet the top of Olympus in June and July. Elsewhere, broom is big and prickly, up to 2m/6ft high. After blossoming in March and April, its flower shoots harden into thorn spikes.

Asphodel signals spring, standing a metre high with its white flowers shining in the sun. A yellow version flowers in the mountains. Asphodel has been planted on graves so that spirits may eat its tubers. Those same tubers provide an adhesive used by cobblers - and also as an antidote to diarrhoea.

At Eastertime, bunches of flowering lavender from the lower levels of pillow lava decorate Good Friday processions.

The red-berried *Bosea cypria* catches the eye as it hangs over stony slopes. Eliminated by the Ice Age from the rest of Europe, this shrub survives in only two other places, the Canaries and the Himalaya. It grows between sea level and 700m/2300ft.

Across the island, prevalent drought conditions favour the survival of annual over perennial plants. Corms, rhizomes and tubers are common. Growth resumes with autumn rains, when scilla, grape hyacinth and dwarf narcissi come out, followed by crocus and cyclamen. By April, the countryside is bright with flowers: small blue irises, crocuses and wild tulips. Poppies cover fields with red, yellow, purple. Roadsides are yellow with buttercups, crown daisies, marigolds and huge wild fennel. By June, most have gone.

Stinging nettles spread in summer. Farmers used to dry them to make a protective covering for fruit, vegetables and cheese. Shampoo with a strong infusion of nettles was said to keep dandruff away.

In late autumn, leaves in vineyards turn reddish-orange over large areas.

Forest law forbids picking or cutting any plants.

TREES

Ancient writers described Cyprus as green and heavily forested. Today, 19% remains under timber. Fire, exploitation and neglect have denuded and eroded some highland areas. Air attack burned one-fifth of the forests during the 1974 Turkish invasion. Nevertheless, ancient forests survive, thanks to good management and hard work by the Forestry Department. Around their station at Stavros tis Psokas, 30,000 cedars fill the valleys.

The Mount Olympus region is a National Forest Park. Black pine (*Pinus nigra*) is widespread above 1200m/4000ft. It spreads through its root system, helping regeneration. Some massive specimens are centuries old. Those that avoid lightning strike can reach 15m/50ft in height. Among the pines are stands of juniper (*Juniperus foetidissima*).

Aleppo pine (*Pinus brutia*) covers lower Troodos. The leaves are bright green needles and its reddish cones hang on for years. The tree is tapped for resin and its timber was valuable to builders of ships and houses.

Evergreen dwarf golden oak is endemic from 800m/2600ft up to 1800m/6000ft on the igneous rocks of Troodos and elsewhere on Cyprus. More of a bush than a tree, its leaves are greenish orange on one side, light yellow to brown on the other.

Undergrowth is thick in the forests as the intense sunlight penetrates the tree cover. Red-barked strawberry trees reach 5m/15ft. Lower bushes of rock-rose flower in April and May. Annuals and perennials flower at ground level.

The cypress tree towers over cemeteries. Hedges of its dense dark-green foliage make windbreaks for plantations. Cypress cones provided another herbal remedy and the wood made good furniture.

Non-native species are being systematically naturalised, including big American sequoia trees, palms, mimosa, jacaranda and bougainvillea. Stands of bamboo and groves of banana grow well. Citrus fruit trees came from China as an Arab import. The British brought the eucalyptus from Australia. Aphrodite herself is credited with introducing the pomegranate, now a common hedge plant. Its ripe red fruit is still splashed outside some newly wed homes as a symbol of fertility.

Olive and carob trees grow widely in the hot, arid conditions. A sacred tree in Greece, the olive has a clumpy top on a twisted silver-grey trunk. Its fruit is a staple in the Mediterranean diet, also providing cooking oil and herbal ointment. Try a sandwich of Cyprus bread, spread with olive oil and filled with olive fruit. Mind the stones. The wood makes good charcoal.

Carobs are big trees with thick dark trunks and leathery leaves. The brittle pods make a valuable harvest, providing chocolate flavouring, a sugary syrup, cosmetics, pig food - and material for photographic film. John the Baptist ate them when in the wilderness, hence the name St John's Bread. That's not all. The hard seeds, of uniform size, were the original goldsmith's carat weight.

The maquis is a deforested region. Golden oak, juniper and strawberry trees grow on upland maquis in the Troodos foothills and parts of Akamas. The lower maquis slopes of Akamas, around Stavros tis Psokas and above Pafos, support lentisk, wild olive and carob trees. Gorse and thorny broom scratch bare legs.

Poor, stony, garrigue lowlands support no crops. Spiny burnet grows well. Besides tearing walkers' legs, this prickly shrub made villagers' brooms. But between scattered shrubs, many perennials flower: narcissi, anemone and tulips. Herbs grow here, some culinary like garlic, thyme or marjoram, some medicinal like spurge or borage.

The leafless poplar draws the eye in the winter landscape, its white form shimmering against dark green conifers. River valleys attract other deciduous trees: willow, alder and plane. Myrtle and oleander grow at lower levels.

WILDLIFE

Moufflon sheep wander wild in mountain forests around Stavros. The ram is impressively big, with curved horns curling protectively over the neck. Hare and fox, even an occasional hedgehog, may be seen in the mountains.

REPTILES

Legend links Cyprus with reptiles. It was once known as Ofioussa, the home of snakes. Seven species survive, including various whip snakes. Some of these are large, but harmless to humans. The Balkan whip snake doesn't undulate - it glides around olive groves and vineyards. Another whip snake is the largest in Europe, growing to 3m/10ft. It likes open countryside in maquis and garrigue regions. If disturbed, it coils up and hisses loudly. Ravergier's whip snake likes stony ground and walls.

The venomous blunt-nosed viper has a head distinct from its neck. It likes dry water-courses with a few wet spots. Also poisonous to people, the Montpellier snake escapes from their approach at high speed. The rare cat snake has a mouth said to be too small to bite a human.

Snakes are active from March until autumn when they hibernate in stone walls or rock crevices. They shelter in similar places from excessive heat. Some seek water to help shed skin. Although field workers still wear high boots for protection, walkers are not likely to see snakes. But don't walk barefoot and don't rummage around in rocks.

Lizards run everywhere. The big, shy, dark olive starred agama, looking like an iguana, grows to 30cm/1ft. Chameleons are not uncommon.

BUTTERFLIES

Fifty different species of butterfly bring colour to the air of Cyprus. Most appear in spring. Some, notably Red Admirals, fly until late December. Many are endemic, some very local. Migrants arrive - sometimes clouds of them - from Africa. They fly to Europe in relays, reproducing the species en route.

BIRDS

Following a main migration route, millions of birds visit Cyprus each year. Millions more winter and breed here. Watchers have recorded 357 species, of which 50 are permanently resident. 27 of the migrant types stay to breed.

From August, storks and cranes stop overnight, on their way south to Egypt. Many raptors pass through in autumn. Flamingoes fly in from the north in November. They share Larnaca and Akrotiri salt lakes through the winter with egret, ibis and heron as well as ducks and geese.

Spring is the best season for bird-watching. Northbound swallows arrive in mid-February: some people date their first arrival precisely on the 19th. Bee-eaters, golden oriole, hoopoes and rollers bring exotic colours.

Eleanora's falcon arrives in April and breeds on the Akrotiri cliffs. Nightingales nest on the southern Troodos slopes and sing all round Platres. Scops owls chirrup away up there as well.

Named as the national bird, the little Cyprus warbler resembles the Sardinian warbler.

HISTORY

The earliest known map showing Cyprus dates back to 500 BC, but people have lived on the island for over 7,000 years. From 5800 BC to 3000 BC they occupied the oldest settlements yet discovered, at Khirotikia, between Limassol and Nicosia. Copper workers came to Lemba near Pafos around 3500 BC.

Trade in copper and timber attracted settlers from Greece. They brought their own language, religion and social patterns. Phoenician immigrants added their influence. City-states grew up, with local kings. By the 3rd century BC, the original Eteocypriot stock had virtually vanished.

During those centuries, foreign rulers came and went. Strategically placed between Europe, Asia Minor and Africa, the harbours of Cyprus caught a number of imperial eyes, starting with the Pharaohs.

In 330 BC, Cypriot ships helped Alexander the Great expel the Persians; Alexander's own fleet was built of Cypriot timber. Two stable centuries of Hellenic civilisation followed.

Shortly after the Romans came in 58 BC, St Barnabas and St Paul brought Christianity. After three centuries of Roman peace, order and culture, the empire split, leaving Cyprus ruled from Constantinople as part of Byzantium.

As Cypriots developed their own Orthodox Christian church, their bishops acquired influence and power across the island. Churches spread and numbers grew although belief in the old religions persisted.

Byzantine rule continued from 330 to 1192 AD. But from the 7th century, Moslem expansion challenged Christian control of the Mediterranean. For three centuries Arab raiders sacked and occupied the coastal towns of Cyprus, killing or enslaving the inhabitants.

When European Crusader armies came to fight the Arabs in Palestine, they made Cyprus a base. After King Richard I of England and the Knights Templar, power passed to the French Crusader Lusignan family. Their dynasty ruled in western chivalric style from 1192 to 1489, imposing feudalism and favouring Roman Christianity. They left their mark in the shape of medieval west European architecture, building castles, cathedrals and abbeys.

The struggle between Moslem and Christian continued. The powerful Moslem Turkish empire, the Ottomans, expanded militarily into Europe, capturing the Byzantine capital, Constantinople, in 1453. To keep the Turks out, the Venetians took over Cyprus and built new defensive walls round Nicosia and Famagusta.

But in 1570, the Turks invaded overwhelming the defences. In came Turkish settlers with their own religion, language and culture. Out went alien Lusignan feudalism and the Latin church. And as long as they paid their taxes, the Cypriots kept their own Greek culture and their own Christian church. The bishops sustained both, assuming political and social, as well as spiritual, leadership. For three hundred years, two communities developed side by side, Moslem Turk and Christian Greek. Their different languages even acquired a similar accent, marking both as Cypriot.

After the collapse of the Ottoman Empire in the 19th century, the British took over Cyprus in 1878. In their customary imperial way, they kept the peace, established legal and parliamentary systems and sorted out the taxes which had been Byzantine in every sense.

Memories of the EOKA struggle at Spilia, near the Madari Ridge walk.
(see p.132)

They improved education and health, built 3000 miles of road in 50 years, brought waterpoints to the villages and organised the forestry service. The population tripled.

In the post-colonial era that followed World War II, many Greek Cypriots pressed for *enosis*, union with Greece. Denied this, they achieved independence for Cyprus in 1960, following the EOKA rebellion against British rule.

Turkish Cypriots did the same, rebelling against the new Republic of Cyprus. They occupied the north of the island in 1974 and declared it an independent state in 1983.

APHRODITE

Nobody can move far on Cyprus without hearing the name Aphrodite. She wasn't the first, or only, deity on the island. In the 12th century BC, Cypriots worshipped a god with horns and another who worked copper.

Accounts of Aphrodite's origins vary, but all agree that she rose from the foam of the sea and sailed to Cyprus on a scallop shell. The Romans called her Venus. Another of her names was Kypris, "the Cypriot". She landed near Pafos, at Petra tou Romiou, already a holy place. Cypriots readily adopted this goddess of beauty, love

17

and pleasure.

Grass and flowers grew where Aphrodite trod and wild animals fawned at her feet. She could renew her virginity by returning to the sea at her original shrine.

The handsome hunter Adonis was the favourite among her many lovers. When a boar gored him to death, Aphrodite turned his blood into the red poppies - some say anemones - which still splash the Cyprus hills with colour.

CYPRUS DELIGHT

A Russian traveller disembarked in Cyprus two hundred years ago. Like today's holidaymakers, he didn't know what to expect. Like them, he wrote home about it.

The Russian's name was Barsky. Without maps or signposts, he relied on local guidance in his travels. On foot and mule-back, he reached ancient hillside villages, mountain-top monasteries and the remotest of holy places.

Barsky explored a rich and fertile island which produced fine cheese and butter, fruit and honey, grapes and wines, cotton and silk. Under the earth lay diamonds, gold and silver, copper and iron. Strangest of natural products to Barsky was *lithios amiantos*, "cotton-stone" or asbestos. The island's forest trees grew tall and well grained, making fine ships' masts. Trade flowed through four good harbours. And, to his surprise, there were "not many" brigands.

The people he praised as quick-thinking and eloquent.

In today's Cyprus, walkers share Barsky's surprise and pleasure at their discoveries. They search for ways through deep forested valleys and over rocky peaks. They follow some of the same paths to the same villages and monasteries. They find the same vineyards and orchards, terraces and trees, the same views to the sea.

The mines may be worked out, but mineral workings still dot deserted hillsides. And the "cotton-stone" asbestos excavations at Pano Amiandos dominate the landscape.

Of those four old harbours, Limassol is a major international port as well as a sea-sport centre. Pafos shelters yachts and local fishing boats. But only Turkish ferries sail from Famagusta and Kyrenia, occupied since 1974.

WHERE TO WALK

Away from the capital and the coasts, Cyprus remains a village society, working the land and deeply rooted in the past. Farm tracks skirt hillsides; forestry roads penetrate woodland; ancient mule-trails cross cols and follow ridges. Walkers can try any of them, but without maps or markers, way-finding is difficult.

This book describes day-walks in four regions: the Akamas peninsula, the Pafos hills, Stavros forest, and the Troodos mountains. Some routes are circuits, starting and finishing in the same place. Others are linear walks, needing transport between the two ends.

The Akamas *(ak-ah-mass)* peninsula juts north-west like a rhino's horn. Deep gorges cut across its base and a forested ridge runs to its tip. Rocky hillsides slope down northward to a wide bay. Covering 170sq kms/66sq mls, this westernmost point of Cyprus remains the least-known part of the island. A strong local dialect preserves Homeric echoes in its vocabulary.

Behind Pafos *(pa-foss)*, south-facing hills roll inland. It is country for easy walking through farmed valleys and over open hill-tops. North and east of Pafos, the forested ridges of Stavros remain almost impenetrable.

The Troodos *(troh-doss)* mountains are central to the island. North of Limassol and west of Nicosia, they rise to 1952m/6404ft, with panoramic views. Forestry roads criss-cross the region: their use demands sensible navigational skills. Some tracks have been developed as nature trails with descriptive booklets.

WEATHER

The sun is so consistent that Cyprus sells it as a commodity. From June to September, summers are hot, with clear blue skies. The heated land mass draws in winds, sometimes strong, from the open sea to the north-west. Occasional summer thunderstorms are brief but intense. Summer sea temperatures rise to the mid-20s°C/70s°F.

The inland plain round Nicosia is the hottest spot, with welcome evening breezes in summer. Sea-breezes cool the coasts, especially in the west between Pafos and Polis. Temperatures on Mount Olympus are naturally lower than those on the plain: expect a difference of around 7°C/45°F. Evenings are cool in the mountains.

From November to March, winter weather is less settled, but

still sunny. Rain fills the reservoirs and falls as snow and hail on mountain-tops. The coast is milder than the inland plain. Sea temperatures fall to around 16°C/60°F.

Most spring and autumn days start with brilliantly clear, cloudless mornings. They reach their hottest around mid-day. In the afternoons, cumulus often builds up over mountain-tops for a while. The cloud can bring rain, sometimes heavy, for an hour or so. But expect the cloud to clear, giving brilliant late afternoons and evenings - and colourful sunsets.

In the autumn, afternoons chill down sharply after 3pm. Keen winds cut across Troodos. Darkness - and temperature - fall early and fast. After its winter snows, Mount Olympus can suffer spring hailstorms.

Weather-watchers might like to test some rule-of-thumb tendencies. If the morning starts cloudy, more cloud gathers on the tops. If the day starts clear, it stays clear. A windy start can bring in anything. Pafos people say that the sirocco wind, from the west, is dry; but the levanter, from Limassol and the east, brings rain.

WHEN TO GO

The best months for walking are March to May and September to mid-November. Go in spring for flowers, fruit blossom and Easter processions, in autumn for warm sea-swimming. Night falls early and fast in November: be off the mountain by 4.30pm. The wettest months are December, January and February. The tables give rounded averages as a guide.

| TROODOS: | Temperature | | Sunshine | Raindays |
	Max	Min °C	Hrs daily	per month
January	8	2	4	14
February	9	2	5¼	11
March	12	4	6	9
April	16	7	7¾	6
May	21	11	9½	3
June	26	15	11¼	1
July	28	18	11½	1

August	29	18	$10^3/4$	1
September	25	15	9	1
October	20	11	$7^3/4$	4
November	15	8	$6^1/4$	6
December	10	4	4	12

PAFOS:	Temperature		Sunshine	Raindays
	Max	Min °C	Hrs daily	per month
January	16	8	$5^1/2$	13
February	17	7	$6^1/2$	9
March	18	9	$7^1/4$	7
April	22	11	$8^3/4$	5
May	23	14	$10^1/2$	2
June	29	19	$12^1/4$	0
July	31	21	$12^1/2$	0
August	32	21	12	0
September	30	19	$10^1/2$	1
October	27	16	9	4
November	22	13	$7^1/2$	6
December	18	4	4	12

CLOTHING

In the walking months, dress as for a good southern English summer. The Troodos may wel' be hot, but be ready for rain and chill winds. Pafos and the Akamas are likely to be warm all the time.

The sun is very strong: don't underrate it. Protect bare arms and legs as wel' as head and neck. Remember that many churches and monasteries require visitors of both sexes to cover legs and shoulders.

Shorts can be inadequate on overgrown paths that wind through unyielding low scrub or thorny bushes.

For most of the year, lightweight boots are best. Good trainers are adequate on Nature Trails and earth roads. Even there, occasional rough stretches call for ankle support. In the mud of autumn rains, solid leather is appreciated.

Beyond first-aid kit, no special equipment is needed for these routes. Carry food and plenty of water, refilling wherever possible.

Fit it all, with spare clothing, into a day-pack.

WAY-FINDING

The book's sketch maps were drawn on the spot from observation. Their prime purpose is to illustrate the text. They aim at clarity rather than topographical accuracy. Contours are smoothed out to indicate the general lie of the land rather than to define every indentation. Detail is limited to that which illustrates the route descriptions.

The country is laced with vehicle tracks, too many to map: a compass helps keep a general line of march. There is no systematic waymarking although various organisations have put their own marks along some routes. These may be paint splashes or knots of plastic tape. But positions can be pin-pointed by other useful checks. Numbered concrete bollards mark forest boundaries. Telegraph and power-lines have identity numbers on the poles. Skylined TV masts make useful points to aim for. Where useful, these are mentioned.

Walks in the book use paths or earth roads, providing energetic rather than strenuous activity. There are no scrambles through untracked terrain, although tracks are sometimes on the faint side. Any particularly rough or steep stretches are mentioned. Three grading levels give a rough indication of the demands of each walk: the more difficulties there are, the more stars are shown in the grade.

Some of the best walks are along Nature Trails, marked at each end with rustic shelters or arches, a carved wooden sketch map and leaflet dispensers. These trails are well engineered and maintained, with numbered markers along them. The markers relate to features described in booklets available from Tourist Offices. As local offices run out first, pick the booklets up wherever they are available.

Expect change. Cart-tracks become earth roads; earth roads acquire tarmac surfaces. Farmers' pick-up trucks and tourists' 4WD cars drive new vehicle-tracks into the countryside. Only hunters and hikers remember and use the old paths and mule-trails.

MAPS

The descriptions in the book should be enough to guide walkers along the routes without reference to other maps. For general use, the Bartholomew Holiday Map (£4.99) is clear, showing the whole island at a 1:300,000 scale with topographical colouring. It also has a useful contoured enlargement of the Troodos region at 1:71,500.

For keen map-readers, a 1:50,000 OS-style series, first published in 1973, is available by direct purchase from The Director, Department of Lands and Surveys, Corner Alasias and Demophonton Street, Nicosia, Cyprus.

Ask for Series K717 Topographical Map, scale 1:50,000. The Akamas region is covered by Sheets 8 and 16; Pafos by 16 and 17 (and a bit of 22), Stavros by 9; Troodos and Olympus by 18 (plus 19 for Madari and Papoutsa). The cost of one sheet in 1994 was CY£3.00 plus VAT @ 8% plus packing and airmail postage: say £5.25 sterling. Send payment with the order by standard UK sterling cheque made payable to "Director of the Department of Lands and Surveys, Nicosia".

DEFINITIONS

Route descriptions are in normal type. Extra background information is in italics.

The word "road" is used for any route that can take vehicles. It is further defined by the surface, usually "metalled" for a main road, or "earth" for an unsurfaced cross-country route. "Path" or "track" refers to footpaths, sometimes faint, especially those trodden by hunters. A "mule-track" is usually deeply worn, often looking like a stony stream-bed. "Trail" or "route" means any of these.

A "re-entrant" is a valley closed at one end, between two protruding "spurs", usually cut back into a hillside by a stream. Contouring routes have to hairpin into and out of them. A "gully" is grooved out by water action. A "ravine" is a cleft in a mountainside. A "gorge" is a rocky valley with cliffs as its walls.

Distances and times for each walk figure under the heading "Logistics". Measurements are initially metric, converted into the nearest imperial equivalent. They have been measured on the ground, mostly more than once, on a Silva electronic pedometer which has always proved reasonably accurate. Logistics totals are rounded up.

At the end of paragraphs, the figures in [square brackets] show distances and times since the previous [square bracket]. Sometimes

23

an interim [distance/time] is inserted in the text as an extra check.

Timings are given as an indication of how long to allow. They are based on times actually taken, by groups rather than individuals. They allow for rests and photo-stops. Timings are generous rather than challenging.

In Cyprus, tracks tangle with terraces. Broken landscapes upset any sense of direction. Getting lost is easy. For extra guidance and security, therefore, the route descriptions include compass points. These confirm general directions, especially at track junctions. All that is needed is a reliable, simple compass, clearly showing eight points.

Walk descriptions include drinking-water points, availability of shade, WCs and telephones as well as cafes and shops.

The number of Grade stars indicates the degree of difficulty: distance, gradient, terrain, way-finding.

FOOD

Cypriot dishes are well cooked and tasty. Flavours owe a lot to the island's neighbouring regions, the Levant, Greece and Turkey. Trading partners, as well as occupiers, have also left their traces.

Cooking methods are usually unhurried; meals are best taken at the same tempo.

As the island is self-sufficient in vegetables, cereals and fruit, raw materials are picked fresh each day for the markets.

Walkers in the New Year share the orange and lemon harvest, followed by the first strawberries. From early summer, orchard fruits ripen: apples, apricots, peaches, nectarines, plums, greengages, cherries - large, juicy and sweet. Pomegranates burst in the hedgerows; their juice makes an iced drink. Walkers in late summer and autumn enjoy figs and dessert grapes. Water melons cool the thirst.

Cooks find their herbs on the hillsides, not in little bottles. Food flavours come from local bergamot and borage, marjoram and myrtle, mint and fennel, sage, rosemary and thyme.

Cypriot cooks know all about vegetarian dishes, which come to the fore on Orthodox Greek menus during the fifty days of Lent. Vegetarian visitors reap the benefit all the year round with stuffed tomatoes and peppers, aubergines, avocado pears and artichokes.

Pitta bread comes filled with red pumpkin and raisins *(kol-oh-kee tho pee-ta)*, or egg and spinach *(spa-nah-koh pee-ta)*.

For a cheap light lunch, ask for a village salad *(salata horry-ah-tee-kee)*. The nearest to fast food is a kebab sandwich in pitta bread. Some market stalls sell rolls with an olive and onion filling; or cheese pasties; even local sausage rolls. Eggs for village omelettes are laid by hens fed as nature intended, out of doors.

Look-ah-nee-koh is a Cypriot sausage, rich in meat, smoked with spices and soaked in red wine. Many villages have specialities, like *ja-la-tee-nah*, bits and pieces of pork in their own jelly, flavoured with pepper and bay. Pork and lamb are favourite meats. Goat tastes stronger than lamb.

On a cool evening, ask for soup, especially in a village family restaurant. *Av-go-lem-ono* features chicken with lemon, egg, rice: it is an Easter favourite. For vegetable soup, ask for *hort-oh-soopa*. *Rev-ith-ia* is made with chick-peas. *Tra-ha-na* adds yogurt to cracked wheat.

Each restaurant has its own mix of *mez-ess*, a rich collection of appetizers: savouries, smoked ham, meat and squid. *Mezes* can also be a main meal, with a dozen or so plates in hot succession. Serious eaters pace themselves to extract full enjoyment.

Dips are on the table: *ta-hee-nee* (crushed sesame seed paste), *ta-ra-mo-sa-la-ta* (smoked cod roe with lemon juice, garlic and olive oil), *ta-la-tour-ee* (yogurt and cucumber).

Cypriot seas are not the best of fishing-grounds, but *sfee-ree-dah*, sea-bass, is good - as is *ksee-fee-ass*, fresh swordfish. *Barb-oo-nee* is red mullet, *fang-ree* sea-bream. Octopus in red wine is *octa-poh-dee krass-ah-toe*. *Mar-ee-da* are like whitebait. Trout farms are a thriving local industry.

Look for these words on menus, sometimes with varied spellings:

afelia	Pork marinated in red wine with coriander and slowly stewed
avgolemono	Chicken soup with lemon, egg, rice
bourekia	Minty cheese and ravioli in pastry, enjoyed just before Lent
dolmadhes	= *koupepia*
hiromiri	Leg of pork, spiced and marinated in red wine, pressed and smoked

hortosoupa	Vegetable soup
houmous	Chick-pea puree
kalamari	Squid
karaoli yackni	Snails in tomato sauce
keftedes	Meat balls
kleftiko	Chunks of meat and veg roasted in their own juices in a sealed outdoor oven
kolokassi	Like sweet potato, stewed with pork
kolokopitta	Pitta bread filled with red pumpkin and raisins
koupepia	Rolled vine leaves, stuffed with minced meat and rice
loukaniko	Smoked spiced sausage
lounza	Smoked fillet of pork
louvia me lahana	Greens and beans in oil and lemon
melintzanes yahni	Baked aubergines and fresh tomatoes
mezes	Long series of savouries
moussaka	Layers of fried aubergine, potato and minced meat, casseroled in wine and often served in individual pots
pougouri pilaf	Fried onions, cracked wheat and chicken stock, steamed together, plus yogurt
revithia	Chick-pea soup
salata horiatiki	Village salad
sheftalia	Grilled rissoles
souvlakia	Charcoal-grilled lamb and vegetable kebab - traditionally the first big meal after Lent
spanakopitta	Spinach, cheese and egg pie
stifado	Beef, veal or hare stewed in wine with onions
tahini	Dip of crushed sesame seed paste
talattouri	Dip of yogurt and cucumber
taramosalata	Dip of smoked cod roe
tavas	Lamb or beef, casseroled with its vegetables in an earthenware pot
trahana	Cracked wheat soup with yogurt
tyropitta	Cheese pie
yemista	Stuffed vegetables with tomatoes, onions, courgettes, peppers, aubergines, marrows
zalatina	Pork in jelly, like brawn.

Don't expect a pudding; just enjoy the fruit:

akladia	Pears
damaskina	Plums
glyko	Fruit preserved in syrup
kerasia	Cherries
meela	Apples
portokahlia	Oranges
seeka	Figs

Sweetmeats from cake shops are mostly very sweet:

baklava	Almonds, cinnamon and lemon syrup in pastry layers
bourekia tis anaris	Sugared pastry filled with cream cheese and honey
daktyla	Almonds in pastry
galatoboureko	Pastry and creamy semolina
halva	Sesame seeds and honey
kadayfi	Syrupy shredded wheat
loukoumahdes	Honey-soaked doughnuts - popular at Epiphany, 6 January
vasilopitta	Cake for St Basil's day - 1 January

Resort restaurants cater cheaply and well for basic British tastes, some even serving rice-pudding: *rizogalo*.

Most restaurants add a service charge, VAT and a CTO (Tourist Office) tax: it's shown on the menu.

Hotel breakfasts are of continental style; eggs cost extra. Knowing their clientele, many town cafes offer a big British breakfast.

Food minimarkets sell standard provisions for walkers, including rye-biscuits. Most sell wrapped imported cheeses. *Halloumi* is a firm cheese from Cypriot ewe's milk. *Kefalotiri* and *kashvali* are hard cheeses; *fetta* is soft and salty. For a trail snack, chew *pastellaki* - ΠΑΣΤΕΛΛΑΚΙ - made of sesame seed, peanuts and carob syrup.

DRINK

The vineyards of Cyprus have a distinguished 4,000 year history, featured on early coins, pottery and mosaics. The earliest recorded export of wine was in 900 BC.

King Solomon sang about Cypriot wines; the Pharaohs drank them; Greeks and Romans praised them. Medieval Crusader kings, even the French, enjoyed them, setting up their own estates of vineyards, the Commandaria.

The name Commandaria passed to the islanders' traditional wine, drunk for centuries as part of the celebrations of Aphrodite. From this history, Cypriots claim the longest pedigree in the world for Commandaria. Its red grapes come from a limited region of eleven villages on the southern Troodos slopes. Only one village, Chalochorio, can sell Commandaria direct to the public.

Picked late and dried for 10-15 days under an intense sun, the fruit is sweet and well flavoured. Fermentation was traditionally in open earthenware jars, never quite emptied. Continuity remained unbroken as the old residue fermented the new. The jar was called *mana*, mother. A long maturation produced a distinctive rich red, sweet dessert wine.

Village tavernas serve village wines, fermented locally from local grapes. Very cheap, they are almost always worth trying.

Wines in larger restaurants and shops are good and varied and still reasonably priced. Light dry whites include Amathus, Arsinoe and White Lady. Aphrodite has a fuller body and flavour. Bellapais sparkles. St Hilarion and Saint Panteleimon are sweeter whites. The Kolossi label covers a red and a white, both well flavoured with firm bouquet. Afames and Othello are full reds; Olympus is softer.

Four major producers - Keo, Sodap, Etko and Loel - set the standards and open their wineries for visits and tastings. Limassol stages a popular Wine Festival in September.

These wineries buy their grapes from thousands of private vineyards, covering 8% of the island area and employing 8% of the labour force. Wine grapes grow in strictly limited regions behind Limassol and Pafos on stony terraces, drawing water from sub-strata. The grapes are usually black Mavro or white Xynisteri, both native to Cyprus, although other varieties have been introduced. Westward from Limassol, vineyards on the rich, well watered soil of the coastal strip produce dessert grapes.

Independent wineries in the Krassachoria district south of Mount Olympus produce good distinctive wines of the region. Look for the names Omodos, Kato Platres, Koilani or Arsos.

With Cypriot brandies, people tend to get what they pay for. A glass of "Five Kings" usually goes down well.

A local lager is brewed by Keo. It is often available only in litre bottles. Carlsberg is also brewed on the island.

Stin-ee ya sass is the toast. Or, briefly, *Stin!* An invitation to drink is *Kopiaste.*

Shops sell bottled water and boxed fruit juices. In season, orange juice is squeezed directly into the glass. Soft drinks are the standard internationals, or sweet fruit fizzes.

Coffee is either Nescafé *(nes)* or thick, black Cyprus coffee. Don't call it Turkish. This is boiled in *imbrikia*, individual copper pots, until it froths. Specify sweetness with the order, as sugar goes in early: *skeeto* says no sugar, *met-rio* medium-sweet, *gleekee* sweet. A glass of cold water comes with Cyprus coffee to offset its strength.

Tea comes from a familiar pot, or tea-bag - but tea buffs can savour local herbal brews. Say *hamo-meelee* for camomile and watch it being simmered up from brittle dry leaves picked on the mountainside.

GETTING THERE

Carry a full passport. No visa is needed for EU, most other European, Commonwealth, US nationals (1994). Previous entry-stamps to Turkish-held Cyprus can hinder admission. Fly to Larnaca or Pafos airports, or take a ferry-boat from Greece, Israel, Italy or Egypt to Limassol.

At 1994 sterling prices, a seat-only return flight from the UK costs anything from £150 to £350. With a hire-car, this gives most flexibility, but availability is limited.

For the cheapest option, take a package holiday in Limassol or Pafos, with hire-car. With an early start, walking is accessible from either centre. Troodos is an hour's drive from Limassol, the Akamas an hour from Pafos.

A week's bed and breakfast in the walking months costs about £225 per person, plus under £100 for a hire-car. Out-of-season apartment prices can be very reasonable. Hotel packages in the Troodos are nearer the £400 mark. A spring or autumn package holiday for a week, self-catering in Lachi on the Akamas coast, costs about £240, plus car.

Village Bedford bus serving Kilani and Omodos

LOCAL TRAVEL

Regular bus and taxi services are listed in a leaflet, Domestic Transportation Services Itineraries and Tariffs. Ask the CTO for a current copy.

Transurban bus services link the major towns. Faster and more frequent are Transurban taxis, where travellers ring a local number to book a seat. These shared taxis pick up and drop off as wished within the towns.

Larger towns have the usual local bus services: ask for the timetable at the local CTO Office. Urban taxis charge by meter.

Many villages have their own bus, often a veteran Bedford, providing an early run into town.

Walkers find Rural Taxis useful. Drivers are helpful and often interested in walkers. Based in villages, they charge fixed rates based on distance (1993: 17c per km). If in doubt, give them a clearly printed note of a pick-up place and the time for the end of a walk. There is a charge for waiting time (1993: CY£1.75 per hour). Tips need not be extravagant but are appreciated.

Rental cars, motor-bikes, scooters and mopeds, complete with insurance, are on competitive offer in every town. Hirers must show their current UK licence. Look for special deals by arranging the hire with the holiday booking. That way, the small print is available in advance.

Road signs are in Greek and English, with distances in kilometres. Drive on the left. Normal speed limit is 80kph/50mph; motorway speeds have to be between 100kph/60mph maximum and 65kph/40mph minimum. Wearing front seat belts is compulsory; helmets are required on motor-cycles. Police enforce strict drink-driving laws.

All grades of petrol are available, including unleaded. Keep an eye on the gauge, as pumps are still thin on the ground out in the country. Many petrol stations have 24hr automatic dispensers, accepting notes.

ROAD DISTANCES

	Nicosia	Limassol	Pafos	Platres	Polis
Approx.	*kms/mls*	*kms/mls*	*kms/mls*	*kms/mls*	*kms/mls*
Nicosia		75/47	150/93	91/57	185/115
Limassol	75/47		71/44	44/27	103/64
Pafos	150/93	71/44		62/39	35/22
Platres	91/57	44/27	62/39		80/50
Polis	185/115	103/64	35/22	80/50	

WHERE TO STAY

Coastal resorts have year-round hotels, apartments, youth hostels and licensed campsites. Hotel charges are for the room. Winter prices are cheaper.

Campsites are licensed by the CTO and provide showers, toilets, food. Users are charged for the tent plus each person in it. 1992 prices: CY£1.50 per tent + CY£1 per person. Wild camping is forbidden in the forests - ask locally for alternatives. Sports shops sell camping gas cylinders.

Most large Troodos villages have inexpensive hotels. Platres has several at all price levels. Some close in October, re-opening for the ski-ing season. Troodos youth hostel is open in July and August: tel. (05) 421649. The campsite opens from April to October: tel. (05) 421624.

Pafos youth hostel is open all year at 37 Eleftherios Ave, tel. (06) 232588.

Polis campsite is in a eucalyptus grove by the beach. Open March to October: tel. (06) 321526. The nearest site to Pafos is 3kms/1¹/₂mls east on the coast at Zenon Gardens. Open April to October: tel. (06) 242277. Another is 16kms/10mls north, at Coral Bay. Open all year: tel. (06) 621534. Governor's Beach site is 20kms/12¹/₂mls east of Limassol. Open all year: tel. (05) 632300.

Deep in the forests west of Kykkos is a Forest Station at Stavros tis Psokas. It has a Rest House, a campsite and a cafe. Book ahead for accommodation. Given a day's notice, the cafe owners prepare sandwiches and cook meals. They sell drinks but not picnic foods or fruit. Tel. (06) 332144 or (06) 722338.

Some monasteries provide simple overnight accommodation for men only. Check at the nearest CTO Information Office.

Personal Responsibility
This book offers guidance on walking in Cyprus.

Walkers still have to take their own responsible decisions and make their own local enquiries relating to safety or well-being.

SOME PHONETIC GREEK
Useful books:
Gambarotta & Scamp, *Breakthrough Greek*, Macmillan, £9.50; with 3 necessary audio cassettes, £35.
Linkword Greek, Corgi, 1992, £4.99.
Words and phrases: *Greek Travelmate* , £1.

The approaching person usually speaks first:

Good day: *Kali mehra*   Good evening: *Kali spehra*.
Hello: *Yah-soo* to one person; but say *Yah-sass* to more than one person, or to be extra polite.
To a greeting including *Kalos* (*kalos orisateh* or *kaloston*), reply *Kah-loss-ass vree-kah-meh*: pleased to meet you.
Add-ee-yassass is a polite farewell. Cheerio: *Ya harah*.

Androlikou, a deserted Turkish village in the Akamas
Cover from the sun among rocks on the Akamas coast path

Approaching the Baths of Aphrodite from the Akamas coast path
Walking east on the Akamas coast path

Excuse me is *See-noh-mee*.
Yes is *Neh* and No is *Okhee*.   For OK, say *En daxi*.
Please after an enquiry is *Para-kaloh*.
Thank you is *Ef-harees-toh*, acknowledged by *Para-kaloh*.

near:	*kon-dah*	far:	*mac-ree-yah*
up:	*pah-noh*	down:	*kah-toh*
here:	*eth-oh*	there:	*ek-ee*
left:	*areester-ah*	right:	*thexee-yah*
straight on:	*kat-eff-thee-ah* or *ish-yah*		

Half-hour:	*mee-see ora*	One hour:	*mee-yah ora*
It's cold:	*ehee kr-ee-oh*	It's hot:	*ehee zess-tee*

My car's broken down: *hal-asseh toh afto-key-nee-toh* moo.

Notices

ΑΠΑΓΟΡΕΥΜΕΝΗ ΠΕΡΙΟΧΗ ΚΥΝΗΓΙΟΥ = Game Reserve. No Hunting.

ΑΠΑΓΟΡΕΥΕΤΑΙ Η Η ΚΑΤΑΣΚΗΝΩΣΗ ΕΝΤΟΣ ΤΟΥ ΔΑΣΟΥΣ = No Camping in the forest.

Alphabet

Stress the first syllable on all except *om-egga*.

A	α	alpha	=	a		
B	β	beta	=	v		
Γ	γ	gamma	=	g		
Δ	δ	delta	=	d		
E	ε	epselon	=	e		
Z	ζ	zeeta	=	z		
H	η	eeta	=	i		
Θ	θ	theeta	=	th		
I	ι	yota	=	i		
K	κ	kappa	=	k		
Λ	λ	lamda	=	l		
M	μ	mee	=	m		

N	ν	nee	=	n		
Ξ	ξ	ksee	=	x		
O	o	omeekron	=	o		
Π	π	pee	=	p		
P	ρ	roh	=	r		
Σ	σ	seegma	=	s		
T	τ	taf	=	t		
Y	υ	eepseelon	=	i		
Φ	φ	fee	=	f		
X	χ	key	=	h		
Ψ	ψ	psee	=	ps		
Ω	ω	omega	=	o		

ALPHABETICAL FACTUAL INFORMATION

Air Travel - Nearly thirty airlines operate scheduled and charter flights into Larnaca and Pafos. Flying time between Cyprus and UK is 4½hrs; Germany, France, Netherlands 3½hrs; Switzerland 3hrs; Sweden 5hrs; Greece 1¾hrs.

Larnaca Reservations Office: (04) 654294. Buses run between airport and town (5kms/3mls: 25c). Distance from Larnaca to Limassol 70kms/44mls, Nicosia 49kms/31mls, Pafos 139kms/89mls.

Pafos Airport Information: (06) 236941; Reservations Office: (06) 233556/233749. No bus service to town: just taxis (15kms/9mls: CY£5 per vehicle). Packaged holidays provide transport. Distance from Pafos to Limassol 63kms/39mls, Nicosia 146kms/91mls, Polis 50kms/30mls.

Antiquities Department - administers museums and ancient sites. 1 Museum Street, Nicosia, tel. (02) 302189.

Bank and Public Holidays - 1 January, 6 January (Epiphany), 25 March (Greek Independence Day), 1 April (EOKA Day), Easter week-end including Monday, 1 May (Labour Day), 15 August (Assumption), 1 October (Cyprus Independence Day), 28 October (Okhi - Greek National Day), 25 and 26 December. Public services, shops and offices shut. Some resort shops stay open.

Banks - open on weekdays from 08.30 to 12.30 and on Monday afternoons. Some offer afternoon opening for tourists. They are not generally busy at opening time. All exchange both banknotes and travellers' cheques. Some have external Visa cash outlets for those with PIN as well as card. Airport banks stay open all day and for night flights. Some villages have a bank, often with limited opening days.

Books - Available in Cyprus:
Adrian Akers-Douglas: *Discover Laona*, CY£2.50.
Christos Georgiades: *Nature of Cyprus*, 1989, CY£4.50.
Kevork K Keshishian: *Romantic Cyprus*, 1992, CY£7.
Bill Oddie & Derek Moore: *Birdwatchers' Guide to Birds of Cyprus*, 1993, CY£3.50.
George Sfikas: *Birds & Mammals of Cyprus*, 1992, CY£3.50.
Valerie Sinclair: *Floral Charm of Cyprus*, 1991, CY£7.95.

A. & J. Stylianou: *Painted Churches of Cyprus.*
Available in UK:
Cyprus, Insight Guides, 1993, £12.99.
Cyprus, Nelles Guide, 1993, £8.99.
Mark Dubin: *Cyprus*, Rough Guides, 1993, £8.99.
Colin Thubron: *Journey into Cyprus*, Penguin.

Cats - Returning from Palestine with a fragment of the True Holy Cross, St Helena found Cyprus infested with snakes. She tried to establish an ecological control by disembarking a shipload of cats at Cape Gata on the Akrotiri peninsula (*gata* is Greek for cat). The monastery there is still called St Nicholas of the Cats.

Churches - are often locked. Ask for the key at the nearest house or cafe. The keyholder appreciates a little offering. A torch and binoculars help see into dark corners. Dress modestly, covering legs and shoulders. 10% of the island's 5,000 churches still have their original frescos and icons. The icons hang beyond a low rail or screen; foreigners should not pass this. In some churches, wax models represent a person or a limb needing remedial attention from the resident saint.

Credit Cards - are accepted in town shops and hotels. Cash dispensers in towns can be operated with standard Visa or Master cards and PINs, debiting accounts at home. The current (1994) charge is 1.5% of the sum drawn.

CTO - Cyprus Tourist Organisation.

Currency - A Cyprus pound breaks down into 100 cents. Banknote denominations are CY£20, 10, 5, 1 and 50c. There is a limit on how much Cypriot currency can be imported to the island (CY£50 in 1994), but no limit on other currencies. In 1994, £1 sterling bought CY£0.73c.

Cycles - including mountain bikes, can be rented in coastal resorts and Platres. Most roads are quiet and there is enormous potential for rough-riding. Mountain bikes could be used on most of the earth road routes in this book, but not on Nature Trails, which are strictly for walkers. Beware of the sun, heat and dehydration.

In Troodos, the Jubilee Hotel operates a Mountain Bike Centre, providing maps and advice. Bike rental in 1994: CY£18 per week, + CY£25 deposit. The Cyprus Cycling Federation organises events: 20

Ionos Street, PO Box 4572, Nicosia, tel. (02) 456344.

Demons - or *kalikandjari* traditionally came to earth at Christmas and terrorised people for twelve days, until Epiphany. As the demons lived on the roof-tops, people tossed pancakes up there on Epiphany eve so that they left in a happy frame of mind. Two common flowers kept them at bay: St John's Wort and fennel, hung from the rafters with its seed stuffed in keyholes.

Dogs - are seldom seen running loose, probably because strays are put down. They are good at balancing in the back of pick-up trucks from which they bark at walkers. There is no rabies, but it's advisable to go for treatment if bitten.

Easter - Greek Orthodox Easter may differ in date from others. This is the island's major religious occasion. Many parishes carry decorated sepulchres round the village in Good Friday processions. On Easter Saturday, midnight bonfires "burn Judas" outside churches. Postal services are inoperative from Friday to Monday inclusive; food shops open as usual.

Electricity - is 240v, through British-style oblong 3-pin sockets. Don't expect razor sockets in small hotels.

Emergency - In wild country, first contact is most likely to be with forestry officers who have their own 4WD vehicles as well as knowledge of the terrain. Their communications include radio and Forestry Telephones at strategic points. In villages, contact the police.
Ringing 199 gets an immediate English-speaking response covering ambulance, fire and police.
Ring 192 for 24-hour pharmacy service, 104 for road breakdown service.

English-Language Media - The *Cyprus Mail* is published daily in English; the *Cyprus Weekly* on Fridays. British newspapers reach the island within a day. Shops stock books and magazines in English. See also Radio and TV.

Enosis - means union with Greece, the aim of many Greek Cypriots.

Eoka - was the guerrilla organisation that rebelled against British rule. It was led by George Grivas, a Cypriot colonel in the Greek army. Grivas used the name Dighenis, a hero from classical times.

A British viewpoint is given in Laurence Durrell's book *Bitter Lemons of Cyprus* and in a 1966 film, *High Bright Sun*, starring Dirk Bogarde. Other books in English include Charles Foley's *Memorials of Grivas* (Longman) and *Struggle for Cyprus*; *Cyprus Guerrilla* by Doros Alastos (Heinemann); *A Start in Freedom* by Hugh Foot (Hodder & Stoughton).

Festivals - are held on 14 January at Agios Neofytos monastery near Pafos (saint's day fair); 2 February at Chrysorroyiatissa Monastery (Purification of the Virgin Mary); before Lent at Limassol (two weeks of carnival); 23 April at many villages (St George's Day); in May at Pafos and elsewhere (Spring Flower Festivals); in May at Pafos, Polis and other seaside towns (*Kataklysmos* - Festival of the Flood); 15 August at Kykkos and Chrysorroyiatissa monasteries (Assumption); in August and September at many Troodos villages including Agros, Mandria, Moniatis, Foini, Omodos, Platres, Prodromos (Folk Festival), at Limassol for 12 days (Wine Festival), on 8 September at Kykkos, on 20, 21 November at Trooditissa Monastery (Mary in Temple). Check correct dates with CTO.

Fishing - in reservoirs needs a licence issued to personal applicants by the District Fisheries Department in Nicosia, Limassol or Pafos. Sea fishing by line, but not net, is allowed.

Forestry Department - Headquarters at Loucis Akritas Avenue, Nicosia, tel. (02) 302528.
Troodos Divisional Forestry Office: Platania, Prodromos, tel. 02-922454 or 05-421754.
Stavros tis Psokas Station: tel. (06) 332144 or 722338.

Fresco - a religious picture painted with water-paint onto fresh wet plaster on a church wall. The picture dries as an integral part of the wall.

Friends of the Earth - 45 Athanassiou Diakou Street, PO Box 4311, Limassol, tel. (05) 347042.

Gales - hit Cyprus with fairly predictable regularity in autumn and winter. They generally set in from the south-west and veer to the west and north-west. Look out for them around these dates and expect them to last about three days: 27 September, 21 October, 26 November, 6 and 20 December, 11, 19, 28 January, 18 February, 10, 20, 25 March, 29 April.

Geographical Association - 21 Byzantiou Street, Flat 7, PO Box 3656, Nicosia, tel. (02) 368981.

Green Monday - is a family picnic day, before the fifty day Lenten fast.

Health - needs the usual commonsense hygienic precautions. There are no special problems - apart from those self-inflicted, like sunstroke.

Herpetological Society - Mr George Wiedl Hans Jorg, PO Box 2133, Pafos, tel. (06) 238160. Exhibition at Skoulli village, 8kms/5mls south of Polis, tel. (06) 321826.

Hitch-hiking - is permitted. Beware the sun while waiting.

Hospitals - and Rural Health Centres are open 24hrs daily. All except Agros have an ambulance. First aid treatment is free.

Agros RHC	(05) 52137
(limited daytime opening - Kyperounta is nearest hospital)	
Evrychou RHC	(02) 932459
Kyperounta Hospital	(05) 532021
Larnaca Hospital	(04) 630322
Limassol Hospital	(05) 330156
Nicosia Hospital	(02) 451111, 452760
Omodos RHC	
Pafos Hospital	(06) 240111
Paralimni Hospital	(03) 821211
Pedoulas RHC	(02) 952459
Platres RHC	(05) 431324
Platres British Military Hospital	
Polis RHC	(06) 322253
Polis Hospital	(06) 321431

Hunting - The open season runs from 1 October to the end of the year. Shooting wood pigeons is also permitted from June to September. The hunting of permitted game is officially restricted to Sundays and Wednesdays. All this was under review in 1994.

Icon - a holy picture of Christ, the Virgin Mary or a saint, painted onto a panel.

Iconostasis - the screen at the front of a church nave, between it and the sanctuary. Often decorated with icons, all individually done.

Multi-lingual security sign forbidding photography

Language - Greek is the majority language. Many Cypriots speak English very well; most speak it well enough to be helpful. Signs are usually in Greek and English, sometimes Turkish as well.

Laona Project - PO Box 257, Limassol, tel. (05) 369475.

Library Reference - 915.645.

Measurements - are metric. There used to be a Cyprus mile which measured about 3 statute miles. It was the distance a loaded donkey could cover without a stop.

Mosquitoes - still nip, but malaria has gone.

National Forest Parks - The first was Athalassa, near Nicosia. Another is Cape Greco, one of the most beautiful areas of Cyprus, with a short Nature Trail circuit and cycle paths. It is in the south-east corner of the island. Much of Troodos is a National Forest Park, while Stavros tis Psokas is a Forest Nature Reserve. The next Parks are likely to be the Akamas peninsula, Akrotiri and Larnaca lakes and Limassol Forest, 10kms/6mls north of the port.

Ornithological Society - 4 Kanaris Street, Strovolos 154, Cyprus, tel. (02) 420703.

Photography - Equipment, materials, processing and film are widely available in towns. Churches and museums ban flash in case it damages old materials; many allow no interior photography at all. Watch for signs forbidding photography in some areas for security reasons. Most users find a slow film best in the strong light.

Photographic Society: PO Box 2027, Nicosia, tel. c/o (02) 450490, afternoons.

Placename - spellings in English are being standardised. Spellings in this book are taken from CTO maps.

Police - speak English well and are helpful. Emergency phone: 199.

Post Office - hours: Monday-Friday 0730-1330 plus Thursday 1500-1800. Some central town offices open on other afternoons and Saturday mornings. All shut on public holidays. Stamps are also sold in shops: it's quicker to buy them with the postcard.

Radio - in English comes from the 24hr British Forces Broadcasting Service (BFBS) on FM 89.9, 90.5, 92.1, 93, 99.6, with early local weather forecasts.

The World Service is available on MW 227m/1323kHz and SW 6.195, 12.095, 17.640.

Cyprus Radio broadcasts English-language news and weather forecasts on FM 91.1 and MW 498m/603kHz at 10am, 2pm and 8pm.

Check details in the *Cyprus Mail*.

Railway - Services ran between Famagusta, Nicosia, Morfou and Evrychou from 1905 until closure in 1951. The steam trains linked about twenty villages, carrying passengers, animals and minerals.

Riding Stables - Limassol, Nicosia, Pafos, Troodos.

Road Walkers - should keep to the right and face oncoming traffic.

Sea Sports - at all coastal resorts include canoeing, parascending, sailing, scuba, water-ski, windsurfing. Aqualung fishing must be licensed. Recovering antiquities from the sea bed is forbidden.

Shop Hours - October to April: 0800-1300; 1430-1730 (early closing Wednesday, Saturday; closed Sunday). May to September: 0800-1300; 1600-1900 (early closing Wednesday, Saturday; closed Sunday). Chemists open by rota all night and on holidays: details in daily papers, or phone 192. Haggling is not a custom in shops.

Ski - Mount Olympus between January and March. Cyprus Ski Federation, PO Box 2185, Nicosia, tel. (02) 441933.

Snakes - hide from noisy walkers and are seldom seen. Don't disturb piles of hot stones, or walk barefoot. If bitten, go to a Health Centre. Don't attempt to kill or capture the snake, but try to remember what it looked like.

Sub-aqua - Spear-fishing needs a licence. Interference with antiquities and sponges is forbidden. Cyprus Federation of Underwater Activities, PO Box 1503 Nicosia, tel. (02) 454647.

Sunset times -

January 1645hrs	May 1945	September ...1900
February 1730	June 2000	October 1715
March.........1746	July 2000	November ...1645
April...........1915	August 1930	December 1646

Taxes - Prices on labels do not always include VAT (1994 8%). Most restaurant menus add a CTO tax (3%).

Telephones - To call Cyprus from the UK, prefix the full Cyprus number with 00 357.

Bracketed prefix numbers refer to districts within Cyprus. Use them when phoning from one district to another. For local calls within a town or village in Cyprus, omit them. To call the UK from any phone, dial 00 44 + the UK Area Code (omit initial 0) + the number. Or call UK Direct by dialling 080 900 44 and then asking the English-speaking operator for a Collect (Reverse Charge) call to the required number.

Payphones need 2, 10, or 20c coins; new ones take 5c; some work with Cyprus Telecards (CY£2 or CY£5 from post offices or shops). Hotels surcharge phone bills from rooms.

Time - Cyprus is two hours ahead of the UK.

Tips - are appreciated for direct personal service: about 10%. Service charges mean no tip is necessary - but some customers still leave the loose change.

Tourist Office - The Cyprus Tourist Organisation (CTO) has offices in Nicosia, the coastal resorts and airports. The Troodos mountain office in Platres is open from April to late October. Tel. (05) 421316. Cyprus (postal enquiries only): 19 Limassol Avenue, Nicosia, PO

41

Box 4535.

UK: Cyprus Tourist Office, 213 Regent Street, London W1R 8DA, tel. (0171) 7349822.

France: Office du Tourisme de Chypre, 15 Rue de la Paix, 75002 Paris, tel. (01) 42614249.

Germany: Fremdenverkehrszentrale Zypern, Kaiserstrasse 50, D-6000 Frankfurt/Main 1, tel. (069) 251919.

Netherlands: Cyprus Verkeersbureau, Prinsengracht 600, 1017 KS Amsterdam, tel. (020) 6244358.

Sweden: Cypriotiska Statens Turistbyra, Vasagatan 11, S 111-20 Stockholm, tel. (08) 115578.

Switzerland: Fremdenverkehrszentrale Zypern, Gottfried-Keller-Strasse 7, CH8001, Zürich, tel. (01) 2623303.

USA: Cyprus Tourism Organisation, 13 East 40th Street, New York, NY 10016, tel. (212) 683-5280.

Trespass - is not a legal offence, provided there is no damage to land or property.

TV - Channel 2 broadcasts news and weather in English at 2100hrs and relays Euronews from 0700 to 1500hrs daily. Many hotels receive satellite BBC, CNN, ITV, Sky. Check details in the *Cyprus Mail*.

Twilight - is over in 30mins, less in autumn and winter. Be off the hillside in good time.

Walking Holidays - In Cyprus, contact Anthology, 7 Stassandrou Street, Nicosia, tel. (02) 467763 or ask at the CTO. In UK, try Ramblers, tel. (01707) 331133 and Waymark, tel. (01753) 516477.

Water - is claimed to be safe in taps and water points, unless otherwise labelled.

WCs - can be found in most towns and some villages, sometimes in the church grounds. It helps the plumbing to drop paper in the bin instead of flushing it away.

Weather Forecasts - See Radio and TV.

Wildlife Society - PO Box 4281, Nicosia, tel. (02) 303279.

Youth Hostels - in Nicosia, Larnaca, Limassol, Pafos and Troodos are open to IYHA members. Others must buy a guest card on arrival. Cyprus YHA: PO Box 1328, Nicosia.

Akamas Routes

THE AKAMAS PENINSULA

Akamas was one of the Greek warriors who entered Troy in the wooden horse. After the war he settled in Cyprus and was taken by Aphrodite as a lover. Despite a legend that he founded a city here, the peninsula has always been sparsely populated.

Good bases in the Akamas are Polis, Latsi or Drouseia, all with accommodation - or drive up from Pafos in an hour. A frequent daily bus service runs each way between Pafos and Polis covering the 35kms/21mls for 75c. A seasonal bus service links Polis and the Baths of Aphrodite for 45c.

On the still undeveloped and unspoiled peninsula, pine forest alternates with maquis. Steep hillsides, sometimes cliffs, drop to a rocky coastline and clear sea. The creamy limestone surface is patched with pockets of soil reddened by iron. 168 species of bird have been listed, 16 butterfly, 20 reptile and 12 mammal. Of the 530 identified plant species, 33 are endemic and 25 rare. Some botanists believe there are more species still to be discovered.

The Baths of Aphrodite

The Akamas peninsula forms the hilly western arm of Chrysochou Bay. From the cliffs 10kms west of Polis, a tree-shaded pool overlooks the bay. Legend tells that the goddess Aphrodite bathed there.

Steps and a crazy-paved path lead up to the pool and on to the Nature Trail arch. Two trails make a common start of 3kms/2mls, with markers numbered 1-24. The Aphrodite Trail then splits off northward for 4.5kms/2¾mls, with an A prefix to the numbers. Adonis Trail markers, going south for 4.5kms/2mls, are prefixed B. The trails are well trodden and easy to follow, preferably with the free booklet.

There is usually a fruit stall by the arch. Water fountains are decorative but non-potable. Steps lead down to the sea from a changing block and WCs. The Tourist Pavilion is a cafe-restaurant with leaflets. The car park is opposite. Look for a taxi there or telephone from the pavilion.

The Laona Project

Old settlements dot the Akamas peninsula and the Laona plateau across its base. The Laona Project aims to save the area from depopulation and economic decline without damaging its intrinsic character and qualities.

Adrian Akers-Douglas has pioneered an attractive collection of walks and drives on the plateau. Explorers of the locality need his book, *Discover Laona* (CY£2.50), with line drawings and helpful sketch maps.

Priest selling oranges at the Baths of Aphrodite

Akamas altitudes

Drouseia 630m/2070ft
Kathikas 600m/1970ft
Kritou Tera 500m/1640ft
Miliou taverna 200m/650ft
Pano Akourdealia 440m/1445ft
Pano Arodes 590m/1935ft
Old Theletra 350m/1150ft

AKAMAS: WALK 1   Grade ** linear
Drouseia to Latsi via Fasli and Androlikou

North of Drouseia, the flanks of the Akamas peninsula slope down
to the coast. Occasional tiny settlements, some now deserted, dot a
bare, stony landscape. This linear route winds along old earth roads
with frequent sea-views. There is little shade and the tracks are
rough underfoot. The walk divides into sections. From Androlikou
there are two ways to Latsi. These could be linked into a Grade ***
circuit.

Logistics
Start-point: Drouseia.

1.1	Drouseia to Fasli: 4.5kms/2³/₄mls/1¹/₂hrs, down 330m/1080ft.
1.2	Fasli to Androlikou: 2.8kms/1³/₄mls/³/₄hr.
1.3.1	Androlikou to Latsi direct: 7kms/4¹/₂mls/2hrs, down 300m/985ft.
1.3.2	Androlikou to Latsi via Neon Chorion: 9kms/ 5¹/₂mls/2¹/₂hrs, descending 300m/985ft.

Shorter total: 14.5kms/9mls/4¹/₂hrs.

Longer total: 16.5kms/10¹/₄mls/5hrs.

Finish: Return from Neon Chorion or Latsi by taxi.

Or make it a circuit by walking out by the shorter
route and back by the other.

Circuit total: 24kms/15mls/8hrs, down and up 630m/2070ft.
Grade ***

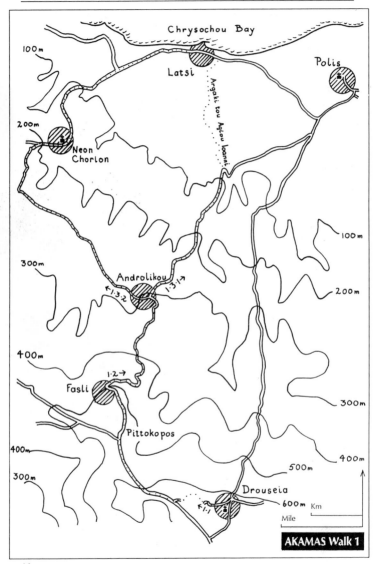

Chrysochou Bay

100 m

Latsi

Polis

Argaki tou Agiou Ioanni

200 m

Neon
Chorion

100 m

200 m

300 m

Androlikou

←1·3·2   1·3·1→

400 m

Fasli   1·2→

300 m

Pittokopos

400 m

400 m

500 m

300 m

Drouseia

600 m   Km

←1·1

Mile

AKAMAS Walk 1

Open-air village oven in Fasli, a deserted Turkish settlement

1.1 Drouseia to Fasli

Start from the crossroads in the middle of Drouseia *(droosha)* (alt. 630m/2070ft), by the church tower and coffee shops. With the church on the left, walk west, downhill. Pass Andros Unisex Hair Salon and the little paved park (WCs) on the right. After a house "Matala", the road becomes a concrete track descending generally north-west through fields. When the concrete ends [800m], take the first fork left up an earth road for 500m to a large rock outcrop on the right. The track veers left to the south-west. Look left for Drouseia's red and white TV mast. 500m from the outcrop, ignore forks right and then left. Make for telephone wires on the skyline and reach a distinct T-junction. Follow two little red arrows pointing right on the facing wall.

[1.75kms/1ml/¹/₂hr]

Descend west-north-west on a rough stony vehicle track between dry-stone walls with the TV mast on the left. This road stretches clearly ahead across the bare countryside, curving from left to right to the skyline and a group of huts. Just after a rubbish tip on the right, join a larger earth road coming in from the left and continue northward to a road fork. Ignore the left fork which descends north-west to Lara and keep straight on through Pittokopos hamlet. 500m ahead, pass a big water cistern ER1954.

[1.75kms/1ml/$^1/_2$hr]

The route follows a well used earth road going north, past a right fork after 500m, to Fasli (alt. 300m/980ft). This deserted Turkish hamlet lies to the left as the track hairpins right.

[1km/$^1/_4$hr]

1.2 Fasli to Androlikou

Follow the well used reddish earth road all the way to Androlikou. Look straight ahead for a chalk ridge. To its left a gully runs north-south with a cluster of houses beyond. At 1.5kms/1ml/20mins from Fasli, the road passes a ruined stone building with an outside oven on the right and crosses to the west side of the north-south gully. Keep northward, past a deserted farm on the left with a collapsed red roof, and a circular concrete water tank dated 1960/1961, into Androlikou *(andro-lee-koo)* (alt. 300m/980ft).

[2.8kms/1$^3/_4$mls/$^3/_4$hr]

Androlikou is a Turkish village deserted since 1974. A few Greek families herd sheep and goats among the ruins. There is no guaranteed drinking water but trees give shade. Near a green telephone kiosk in the centre is a fig-tree, thick in season with luscious fruit.

EITHER 1.3.1 Androlikou to Latsi direct

This route leads directly to Latsi *(lat-see)*. From the telephone kiosk, walk past a street corner door decorated with a wrought iron peacock. Turn right and follow an earth road north-eastward for 4kms. Then descend northward alongside the gorge Argaki Tou Ayiou Ioanni for 3kms into Latsi.

[7kms/4$^1/_2$mls/2hrs]

OR 1.3.2 Androlikou to Latsi via Neon Chorion

To reach Neon Chorion, go north from the telephone kiosk, past an occupied house on the right, and out of Androlikou on the main earth road. After 2kms/1$^1/_4$mls/$^1/_2$hr, pass through a limestone gorge with occupied caves on the right. Ascend west out of the gorge after 200m, on a red road across creamy limestone rock. Fork

Akamas caves used as animal pens and herder's homes

left, north-west, downhill on the red road. The route bears right, northward, zig-zagging up among trees and arable land. It then slips west into and out of a small valley.

An hour after leaving Androlikou, the road hairpins right along the further rim of a wooded valley before running north across a tree-dotted plain. The road twists right, downhill, past a ramshackle collection of sheep-pens, to join a metalled road (alt. 210m/690ft) with a wooden arrow pointing left, westward, to "Smiyies Picnic Site 3k".
[5kms/3mls/1¹/₄hrs]

The route continues on metalled roads. Turn right, descending 1km eastward into Neon Chorion *(nay-o-horry-on)* with a church, cafes and telephone (alt. 150m/490ft). At the north end of the village, fork left downhill, past a Taxi sign on a house, to a road junction signed "Baths of Aphrodite E713 4k; Neokhorio F735 2k; Polis E7133 5k". Keep straight on north-eastward another 1km to the sea at Souli Bar. The coast road leads right, past beaches, to Latsi *(lat-see)* harbour with cafes and shops.
[4kms/2¹/₂mls/1¹/₄hrs]

AKAMAS: WALK 2   Grade ** linear
Neon Chorion to the Baths of Aphrodite: hillside route

From Neon Chorion village, a stony path winds north-westward across the Akamas hillsides. Concealed springs sustain patches of cultivated land among the scrub and trees. Sudden views open out across Chrysochou Bay. This linear route joins the Nature Trail system, giving descent to the sea down an easy footpath, or by steep cliff tracks.

Logistics
Start-point: Neon Chorion (alt. 210m/690ft).
Total distances:

2.1:	5.5kms/3$^{1}/_{2}$mls/2hrs. Down from 210m/690ft to sea-level.
2.2:	10.5kms/6$^{1}/_{2}$mls/3$^{3}/_{4}$hrs. Down from 210m/690ft to sea-level.
2.3:	12kms/7$^{1}/_{2}$mls/4hrs. Down 70m/230ft, up 230m/755ft, down 370m/1215ft to sea-level.

Finish: Baths of Aphrodite: return by taxi.

From the Smiyies Picnic Site sign (alt. 210m/690ft) at the uphill, western, end of Neon Chorion, walk 100m eastward, down the metalled road, past water-tanks on the right, to a road-marker "N.CH 1". Another 50m downhill from this, turn left from the road at Pole PS 85, between new houses. Follow an earth path northward for 15m and fork left, north-west, alongside a stone wall.

After 5mins take the right fork north-westward, ignoring a waymarked track ahead. The path descends north-west to the bed of a small gorge, Arghaki ton Chalavron, and then cuts back north-eastward, out of it. Fork left, and climb a clear path running generally northward. Fork left at a big stone pile, with views over the bay, and continue northward to white Bollard 19, on the right. [2.3kms/1$^{1}/_{2}$mls/40mins]

The next stretch is marked with red/blue waymarks. 700m/5mins on from the bollard, follow them to the right to Bollard 3 on the right. Fork right again to the north-west and follow the red and blue waymarks down a stony zig-zag road. Cross a stream-bed and then ascend 25m to join the Adonis Nature Trail (alt. 140m/460ft). [1.5kms/1ml/¹/₂hr]

From here there are three alternatives:

EITHER **2.1** The shortest and easiest route takes half an hour. Turn right, eastward along the marked trail, following the B numbered markers past B50 for 750m down to the main coast road. Go left for the Baths. [1.5kms/1ml/¹/₂hr]

OR **2.2** Turn left and walk westward on the Adonis Trail, past Marker B49. Follow the B numbers in the reverse direction. After marker B46, make a sharp turn back left, up a steep narrow path. Continue to the unlettered Marker 24 at the Aphrodite/Adonis Nature Trail junction. [3.75kms/2¹/₄mls/1¹/₄hrs]

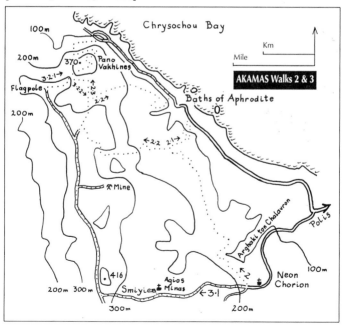

Turn right, following unlettered numbers eastward down a rocky footpath with occasional red spots, cutting across arrowed Nature Trail bends. Rejoin the trail at Marker 18. The path runs clearly ahead, due east toward the sea. After a steep and rocky stretch, the broad track jinks left and right. Zig-zag steeply down the cliff path. At the bottom, turn right, southward, past Marker 6.
[3kms/2mls/1¹/₄hrs]

OR **2.3** Follow Route 2.2 to Marker 24 at the Aphrodite/Adonis junction.
[3.75kms/2¹/₄mls/1¹/₄hrs]

The Aphrodite Trail runs clearly ahead to the north, uphill, for 20mins to Mouti tis Sotiris, the 370m/1215ft summit of Pano Vakhines. Beyond viewpoints at Markers A35 and A37, take 25mins to descend steeply across the seaward hillside, down to a stony coastal road. Turn right, south-east, still following the A numbers, for the Baths.
[4.5kms/2³/₄mls/1¹/₂hrs]

AKAMAS: WALK 3   Grade ** linear
Neon Chorion to the Baths of Aphrodite: Ridge route
See Akamas Walk 2 for map page 51

Follow the forested spine of the Akamas peninsula, with sea-views on each side. Westward from Neon Chorion, the route is easy to follow, passing a remote tiny church on the way. The trail then turns north-west, heading for the peninsula's highest point. A cliff-path leads back to the sea at the Baths of Aphrodite.

Logistics

Start-point:	Neon Chorion.
Total:	15kms/9¹/₄mls/5hrs.
	Ascend 100m/330ft and then descend 300m/985ft to sea-level. Or ascend 170m/560ft and descend 370m/1215ft to sea-level.
Finish:	Taxi back from the Baths of Aphrodite.

3.1 Neon Chorion to the Aphrodite Trail
From the inland, western, end of Neon Chorion, follow the wooden sign "Smiyies Picnic Site 3k" (alt. 210m/690ft) due west on a well used earth road between dry-stone walls. Trees give some shade on the way to the little church of Agios Minas (alt. 250m/820ft) on the right.
[2.25kms/1¹/₂mls/³/₄hr]

St Minas was a Roman soldier, tortured and executed for turning Christian. This monastic church was operated by six monks from St George's monastery near Drouseia. Marks of their cells are visible on the north-east side. The church is a barrel-vaulted 16th century building on 12th century foundations, restored in 1991. Faint remnants of frescos can be picked out.

Pass a Forest Fire notice and fork left, west, uphill past the Smiyies Picnic Site on the right: shade, WCs, water, NT arch (alt. 325m/1070ft). (A self-guided Nature Trail [6kms/3³/₄mls/2hrs] starts here.)

Continue west for another 500m/10mins on a wide stony vehicle track to a triple road junction at a green signpost. A fire-watch station perches high above on the skyline.
[1.25kms/³/₄ml/20mins]

Turn right, ascending northward with sea-views to the left, but no shade. After 1km, pass a right fork signed "Fire Look-Out Station" and bear westward to two Nature Trail arrows marked 9A. Follow "Choice 2 Long Way 5k" straight on for another 500m, past Marker 10 on the left, through intermittent shade. Ignore the first track, contouring away along the hillside to the right. Take the next right, following an unlabelled Nature Trail arrow.
[2.5kms/1¹/₂mls/³/₄hr]

Follow the arrow downhill for 500m, passing a small mining cleft on the right and a house on the left, to an old mine and smelting chimney. Return to the main track.
[1km/³/₄ml/¹/₂hr]

Continue northward on a clear trail along the spine of the peninsula, with fine sea-views to both sides. Over to the right, the old mine is just visible. Reach a military Range Warning flagpole and sign. Far below, a wrecked ship lies on the eastern tip of the cape.
[3kms/2mls/³/₄hr]

Turn right from the flagpole, eastward, for 500m to a fork: each branch of the fork is the Aphrodite Trail, giving two alternative routes.

3.2 Aphrodite Trail to the Baths of Aphrodite

EITHER **3.2.1** To the left, the track is clearly visible, going steeply up Mouti tis Sotiris, the peak of Pano Vakhines (alt. 370m/1215ft). Marker A35 indicates a spectacular viewpoint. From there it drops down the other side to join a rocky coastal road running south-east to the Baths, following A numbers all the way.
[3.5kms/2$^{1/}$4mls/1$^{1/}$2hrs]

OR **3.2.2** The more direct way down is to the right, south-eastward past Marker A30. Just after Marker A25, 1km from the flagpole, the trail forks again. To the right the Adonis Trail goes south, its marker numbers prefixed B.
[1km/$^{1/}$2ml/20mins]

Turn left and descend eastward towards the sea. A rocky footpath, occasionally marked with red spots, cuts across arrowed bends in the Nature Trail, plainly running from Marker 18 toward the sea. After 1km, the broad track jinks left and right before zig-zagging down the cliff-face with some steep steps down. Turn right at the bottom, southward past Marker 6 to the Baths and the Nature Trail arch.
[3kms/2mls/1hr]

AKAMAS: WALK 4   Grade * linear
Akamas Peninsula coastal path

At the centre of Chrysochou Bay, the villages of Polis and Latsi both have beaches, accommodation, food shops, banks and restaurants. Polis has a CTO campsite on the beach, open March to October, tel. (06)321526. Latsi harbour shelters fishing boats and sponge-gatherers as well as a scuba school.

This is a seaside journey all the way. It starts in a boat from Latsi harbour, following the coast north-west to the ancient spring of Fontana Amorosa. A shoreline track continues towards Cape

Arnauti, passing a wrecked ship. The return follows a rocky coastal road to the Baths of Aphrodite. In season the flowers are prolific. Shade is limited and there is no drinking water, even in the Fontana Amorosa. But there is good access to the sea for swimming.

Logistics

Start-point: Latsi.

Boat: 5kms/3mls/³/₄hr.

Total walk: 9.25kms/5³/₄mls/3hrs along the coast path with some ups and downs.

Finish: Return from the Baths of Aphrodite by taxi.

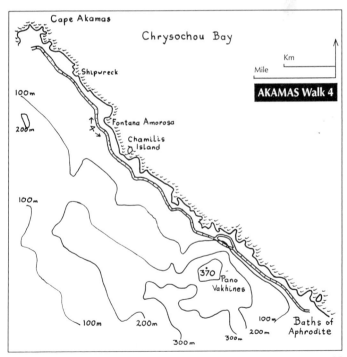

Wrecked ship near Fontana

A full boat costs a few pounds per person. Ask about sharing costs with people taking the boat-trip only. Hire on the spot at the harbour or book in advance through Hans Roelofs at Latsi Water Sports Centre, tel. (06) 321656. He speaks English and German. Some boats have a glass panel in the hull.

400 tombs of ancient burying-grounds lie round Polis. Nearby stood the 7th century BC Greek town of Marion, a copper-trading centre. The staple medieval crop was cotton - and the local wheat was the best on the island.

It's a pleasant boat trip westward from Latsi, past the hillsides below Drouseia, beneath the Baths of Aphrodite and Mouti tis Sotiris peak to Fontana Amorosa *(Loutra Aphroditis)*. Climb out of the boat onto a sandy patch in a little bay. Trees and scrub give shade a few metres above the water. Once a well, the Fontana is marked by a few rocks.

[³/₄hr]

With the sea on the right, walk north-west on an easy track to a wrecked ship. After the wreck, the track veers away from the sea and thick scrub conceals the actual tip of the peninsula. Access to the

sea is easy - over some sharp rocks. Return the same way.
[3.25kms/2mls/1hr]

From Fontana Amorosa, walk south-east on a clear vehicle track with the sea to the left. There is no cliff-edge path. After 20mins pass a Range Warning notice referring to military training areas on the hills above. The road is virtually unshaded but some cover can be found in the scrub round a rocky bay, or, a few metres further on, among the rocks of a little inlet with grey pebbles and a blow-hole.
[2.5kms/1¹/₂mls/³/₄hr]

Orchids thrive along here, flowering with narcissi and cyclamen among the cistus.

The track swings inland round an inlet. It then turns south towards a steep mountain face, which gives shade when the sun is not directly overhead. The track forks, dropping left towards the sea or continuing straight along the contour.
[1.25kms/³/₄ml/¹/₂hr]

The straight one is better, but take either: they rejoin, first at a Nature Trail arch after 250m, again at a Nature Trail arrow near Marker A45. From A45 the route climbs steeply along the mountainside above the sea. After A48, it descends round a corner of the cliff and the Baths come into sight. Take the straight path to the right, down through trees to emerge at the Nature Trail arch.
[2.25kms/1¹/₂mls/³/₄hr]

AKAMAS: WALK 5   Grade ** linear
Drouseia to Lara Bay

Sea-views stretch ahead for most of the way on this easy linear descent westward from Drouseia. An earth road curves round the northern edge of the Argaki tou Pelli valley, reaching the sea at Lara Bay. There are stretches without shade - and no water.

Lara Bay is home to endangered species of turtle which breed there during the summer. A staffed hatchery supervises the region and runs an Information Centre at the north-east end of the beach. The bay is also one of the best swimming spots on the island, with a fine beach, clear water, some shade and not many people.

Between the turtle beach and a cafe, Lara peninsula is a maze of vehicle tracks through scrub. The cafe shuts in October, but provides seats and shade above a shingle beach and a good rendezvous for transport.

Transport back is expensive as the road from Lara to Cape Drepanum is so bad. The alternative is to walk back up the same route.

Logistics

Start-point: Drouseia.
Total: 13kms/8mls/4½hrs, descending 630m/2070ft to sea-level.
Finish: Lara Beach Cafe.

Start from the crossroads in the middle of Drouseia (alt. 630m/2070ft), by the church tower and cafes. Walk west with the church on the left. Immediately fork left up behind the church for 30m. Turn right to walk for 600m westward out of the village. Just past the last house on the right, fork right, north-west. Join Akamas Walk 1 for 1km on the stony vehicle track descending west-north-west. With a signals mast on the left, walk between dry-stone walls, past a rubbish tip on the right. Join a larger earth road from the left and

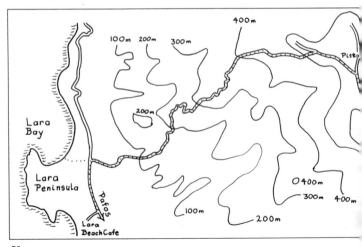

continue northward to the road fork just before Pittokopos (alt. 550m/1805ft).

2.75kms/1³/₄mls/1hr]

Fork left, leaving Akamas Walk 1. A wide earth road descends north-westward to a fork. (The reddish earth road to the right goes north-west along the Akamas peninsula, joining Akamas Walk 3 at the signpost near Smiyies.)

[1.25kms/³/₄ml/¹/₄hr]

Fork left, westward, on a rough limestone road. 10mins later, pass a ruined building on the right and a track left to distant farm buildings among rocks. The only shade on this stretch is 5mins further on, under a fig tree to the left, past a water trough. Stone huts stand on each side of the road 2kms from the Pittokopos fork. Another 1km on, just after a pig-sty on the left, the road dips and forks.

[2kms/1¹/₄mls/³/₄hr]

Keep straight ahead, uphill for a little, following a red arrow on a rock and ignoring the right-hand road. Look left to see Drouseia signals mast on the skyline to the east. Ahead, Lara peninsula juts out from the coast. Olive trees begin to dot the ground and the road passes between a few flat-roofed stone buildings.

[2.5kms/1¹/₂mls/1hr]

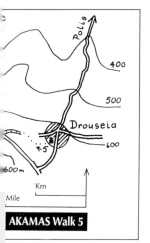

As the country levels out, the north side of Lara peninsula comes into sight ahead. After another 1km through the olive trees, reach the flat coastal strip, marked by a concrete bollard with a red arrow. Fork left, following the red arrow. Pick one of the 4WD vehicle tracks cutting through scrub and head west for the sea. Make a T-junction with the wide, rough but well used coast road. Turn left on it, southward, for a few minutes to a blue "Lara Turtle Hatchery" sign.

Beside it, a gate through a fence leads 100m down to a sandy beach on the north side of the Lara peninsula. There is some shade and excellent swimming.

Follow the earth road south for 1km from the blue Hatchery sign, past another similar sign, to "Lara Beach" cafe.
[4.25kms/2¹/₂mls/1¹/₂hrs]

AKAMAS: WALK 6   Grade *** circuit
Pano Arodes - Three Gorges Circuit

Three hamlets, three ravines and two tiny churches mark the stages on this circuit round the Akamas uplands. Outside the hamlets, walkers could well meet nobody else all day. Easy earth roads lead north-east from Pano Arodes, over uplands to Kritou Tera.

From farmland, the route runs south-east into the difficult wilderness country of Chyparissia gorge: good for birds and seasonal flowers. From a little church on the lip of the gorge, farmers' tracks go south to Pano Akourdaleia. An indistinct path leads down through prickly scrub into another wild gorge and steeply out again.

Country roads return north-westward to Pano Arodes, past a remote church and cave-shrine. Boots and long trousers are advisable. There is shade; but top up water in the villages. Look for orange tape-markers.

Logistics:

Start-point:	Pano Arodes, a half-hour drive from Pafos.
6.1	Pano Arodes - Kritou Tera: 2.5kms/1¹/₂mls/³/₄hr; down 90m/295ft.
6.2	Kritou Tera - Pano Akourdaleia: 6kms/3³/₄mls/2hrs; down 250m/820ft, up 190m/625ft.
6.3	Pano Akourdaleia - Chrysospiliotissa: 3.25kms/2mls/2¹/₄hrs; down 50m/165ft, up 200m/655ft.
6.4	Chrysospiliotissa - Pano Arodes: 1.75kms/1ml/¹/₂hr
Total:	13.5kms/8¹/₂mls/5¹/₂hrs.
Finish:	Pano Arodes.

Alternative start-point: Drouseia.

6.5	Drouseia - Kritou Tera: 3.5kms/2mls/1hr; down 130m/425ft.

6.6	Pano Arodes-Drouseia: 3.25kms/2mls/1hr; up 40m/130ft.
Total:	18kms/11mls/6³/₄hrs.
Finish:	Drouseia.

6.1 Pano Arodes to Kritou Tera

Start at the village crossroads (alt. 590m/1935ft) by a water-point ER 1954 and the road sign "Ineia 4; Drouseia 5; Polis 17".

Walk north in the opposite direction to the road sign arrow, past Pole 4. After 300m on a concrete track, go left on an earth track, north-west between walled vineyards and under a power-line.

A Roman milestone has been found on this track, which runs on to Drouseia.

Fork right at a cross-tracks after 65m, following power-lines north-north-east past Pole 1 and another track from the left. Cross a metalled road and follow the major track uphill north-eastward to

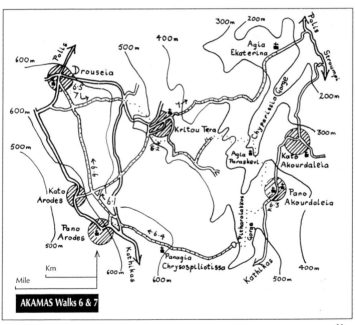

AKAMAS Walks 6 & 7

the highest point (alt. 596m/1955ft). Descend the main track, with views ahead to the sea and a mountainous skyline. Reach Kritou Tera at Pole 50-11 and continue to Pole 50 (alt. 500m/1640ft). [2.5kms/1¹/₂mls/³/₄hr]

Walkers from Drouseia join the route here. To see the village, walk down the narrow street ahead: cafe and shop.

Kritou Tera is one of the Laona villages with a good water supply and a long history of settlement - at least since the Romans. The village springs are just off the main road, near the Royals bus shelter. Holes cut in rock are for laundry work. The mill is now run by electricity instead of water.

6.2 Kritou Tera to Pano Akourdaleia

At Pole 50, turn right, east, up a narrow alley bending between houses to Pole 53. Turn left and follow an old mule-trail south-east out of the village. The trail curves counter-clockwise to a T-junction with an earth road.
[500m]

Turn right, down to a stream-bed. Hairpin counter-clockwise uphill on a concrete surface and take the first fork left onto an earth road running north-east with views ahead to the sea.
[200m]

Follow the broad gravelly road northward uphill. After 700m, fork right at a concrete water-point. Descend south-eastward, curve counter-clockwise round a stream-bed and ascend again. The main track forks right, levels out and curves right downhill from south-east to east. The creamy limestone surface becomes grassy for a stretch. Reach a little plateau where the stone walls end and the Troodos mountains form the skyline ahead.
[1.25kms/³/₄ml/20mins]

The route is straight on, descending steeply due south past a rocky outcrop on the left, down an overgrown track for 150m into a ravine. On the further side of the ravine, a metal pipe runs from right to left. The path into and out of the stream-bed is very rough and steep (alt. 350m/1150ft).

From the ravine, climb straight ahead towards a tree on the immediate skyline. Follow a black plastic water pipe from the tree, north-eastwards along the terraced path, curling round corners up to a flat point at the top, with a dead tree to the left.

Chryselousa church, Pano Akourdaleia

[500m from stream-bed]

The descent now is into Chyparissia - also called Klavaris - Gorge. After 60m, the path turns left. Look ahead to spot the track's zig-zags in a generally northward direction. A grassy stretch varies the otherwise limestone surface. The gorge runs parallel to the track, below and to the right, with the tiny church of Agia Paraskevi on the further side. After 400m, the track splits: go right towards the church for a steep and rough descent with a 20m scramble down to a grassy level. Turn left and keep northward on a clear stony road, curving up, round and down right, past pieces of a ruined water-mill to the stream-bed (alt. 250m/820ft).

[1.75kms/1ml/¹/₂hr]

Partridge and black francolin like the area despite the patrolling raptors.

Walk up to an earth road, turning right for the church.

Agia Paraskevi is only 4m square. Probably built in the 15th-16th century as an estate chapel, it was still used in the 20th century and restored in 1991. It displays the charred remnant of a medieval icon of the Virgin Mary.

Resume the earth road, walking uphill with the gorge to the

right. Long zig-zags lead up to a concrete track into the little village of Pano Akourdaleia at Pole 6 (alt. 440m/1445ft).
[1.75kms/1ml/¹/₂hr]

Pano Akourdaleia has a few score inhabitants. Some of the attra·tive traditional houses are being renovated. Down to the left of Pole 6 is the 16th century church Chryselousa. Opposite is a new church, with a stone press in front and a water tap in the enclosure behind.

6.3 Pano Akourdaleia to Chrysospiliotissa

From Pole 6, turn right and walk uphill through the village for 230m, following the blue Kathikas road sign. Where the earth road bears left, take the concrete track that goes straight ahead, west-south-west, with a wire-fenced orchard on the right. The track runs between vineyards, olive and almond trees for 300m. Where it bends right, leave it and descend straight ahead on a grassy track going south.

Curve round the head of a re-entrant and fork right, downhill, walking west, becoming north-west. The re-entrant opens into a gorge below to the right. Prickly shrubs encroach on the track which curves counter-clockwise, south-west, giving a view to the right over the Pitharolakkos Gorge. Look back to see the sea, before descending south through more prickly broom to the wilderness at the gorge bottom (alt. 440m/1445ft).
[1.25kms/³/₄ml/¹/₂hr]

A hunters' track straggles southward along the bed of the gorge, past an ancient stone trough lying among seasonal wild flowers. Push through scrub for 200m, passing cube-shaped water tanks under the cliff on the right. Just after the third tank, cross a slab over the stream-bed and follow a half-buried metal pipe up to the right for 10m.

This starts the steep climb out of the gorge. A path forks right, away from the pipe, zig-zagging upwards with a low rough retaining wall on its outer edge. It's easier to spot the track from above: look down to check, while keeping generally south-west. Look back across the gorge as well and ascend on a line opposite the end of its bare limestone wall. At this point, the track fades out in a wide

The Avgas Gorge near Cape Drepanon

Orange trees among ruins in the Ezousa valley on the way to Episkopi
Snow can block trails until Easter on Mount Olympus

uphill gully, dotted with scrubby shrubs and trees. Ascend the gully, past patches of old vineyard, looking ahead for shining plastic bags of rubbish just below the skyline. Scramble up past them to a ring of black and white markers round a turning circle at the end of an earth road (alt. 525m/1720ft).
[1km/¹/₂ml/¹/₂hr]

Look north-east to see Pano Akourdaleia, and east to the Troodos mountains. Follow the broad earth road which ascends south-west with the gorge still visible to the left. Ignore side-turnings between the surrounding vineyards. After 700m, cross a crest and see a church ahead, half left. Pass a grape-loading platform and reach the church (alt. 610m/2000ft). It has a water-point outside.
[1km/¹/₂ml/¹/₄hr]

The church, Panagia Chrysospiliotissa (Virgin of the Golden Cave), was built in 1947 above a catacomb, accessible down steps from the south-east corner.

When the Turks occupied Cyprus in the 16th century, they taxed Christians heavily. Many Cypriots pretended to convert to Islam, but secretly continued Christian worship. They were nicknamed "flax-cottons" because they blew with the prevailing wind.

Originally a Greek tomb, then a Roman catacomb, this cave became a clandestine Christian chapel, with an altar against the east wall and remnants of a 14th century fresco on the rock-face. It had its own well. Believers came here to cure damaged eyes with candle soot from the walls.

Legend also tells of the martyr Christina, hidden here from unwelcome Turkish attention. She surrendered herself to save her father from torture; and then poisoned herself.

6.4 Chrysospiliotissa to Pano Arodes

From the loading platform, continue west-north-west on the broad earth road, heading for a skyline mast. After 800m, pass a restored well on the left. Cross a metalled road and follow a concrete track for 400m into Pano Arodes village (alt. 590m/1935ft; cafe, WCs).
[1.75kms/1ml/¹/₂hr]

6.5 Access from Drouseia - Kritou Tera

From Drouseia (alt. 630m/2070ft), walk uphill with the church on the right, past Supermarket Angela, to turn left, east-south-east, at

Christos' Taverna. Follow the Hospital road sign past the Health Centre and school southward out of the village, where the road tarmac gives way to earth [800m]. 50m further on, at an earth crossroads, go left, east, to another crossroads near a power-line junction. Continue south-east, roughly parallel to the power-lines, downhill into Kritou Tera at the cemetery. Turn right and left across the river bed, past a Royals bus shelter uphill, southward, to Pole 50 (alt. 500m/1640ft).
[3.5kms/2mls/1hr]
    Continue as above from 6.2 to Pano Arodes.

6.6 Pano Arodes to Drouseia
From the village crossroads (alt. 590m/1935ft), by a water-point ER 1954 and road sign, walk north in the opposite direction to the road sign arrow, past Pole 4. After 300m on a concrete track, go left on an earth track, north-west between walled vineyards and under a power-line. Cross an earth crossroads after 1km, with the deserted Turkish village of Kato Arodes on the left. Walk between dry-stone walls for another 2kms, cross another earth crossroads and enter Drouseia.
[3.25kms/2mls/1hr]

AKAMAS: WALK 7   Grade * out-and-back linear
Drouseia to Agia Ekaterina
See Akamas Walk 6 for map p61

This out-and-back walk provides a pleasant short day for those based in Drouseia. It passes through Kritou Tera, once a Roman settlement, now being thoughtfully revitalised by the Laona Project. An easy descent leads to a unique church, isolated in open country. Outward views are to the coast at Polis.

Logistics
Start-point: Drouseia.
7.1   Drouseia - Kritou Tera: 4kms/2¹/₂mls/1¹/₄hrs, down
                 130m/425ft.
7.2   Kritou Tera - Agia Ekaterina: 3.5kms/2¹/₄mls/1hr,

down 300m/985ft.
Reverse for the return.

Total: 15kms/9¹/₄mls/4³/₄hrs.
Finish: Drouseia.

7.1 Walk from Drouseia (alt. 630m/2070ft) to Kritou Tera (alt. 500m/1640ft) as in Akamas Walk 6.5.

From Kritou Tera cemetery, turn right and left across the river bed, left at the Royals bus shelter and along a narrow street parallel to the watercourse below. The cafes are at Pole 2 by an outdoor spiral iron staircase.
[4kms/2¹/₂mls/1¹/₄hrs]

7.2 Walk uphill past the shop, out of the village, curving down right past a line of ruined houses. Stay on the metalled road, counter-clockwise round a re-entrant and then north-east down a rocky gorge. Look up left to see Kritou Tera's houses clustered among the hillside trees.

At a green No Hunting sign, the road curves right, through east to south-east. Cross a stream-bed and bear left to the north-east. The metalling has stopped, but concrete stretches cover tight bends.
[1.5kms/³/₄ml/20mins]

As the route inclines further left, to the north, it runs alongside a gorge to the left with the coast visible beyond. Over the hill to the right, out of sight, is Chyparissia gorge. After a steep zig-zag over concrete, the church of Agia Ekaterina comes into sight, ahead and below. The road turns sharply down among vineyards and levels out before the church (alt. 200m/655ft).
[2kms/1¹/₄mls/40mins]

Built as a monastic church in the 15th century, Agia Ekaterina was repaired and restored after earthquake damage in 1953. The building has three aisles, three domes and a series of low arches. It is aligned north-east to south-west. On one wall is a fresco of St Catherine, the patron saint, a Cypriot Christian martyr. The church's water supply was laid on by Dighenis in one of his legendary achievements.

7.3 Reverse the route to return.

AKAMAS: WALK 8
Miliou circuit via Old Theletra

Grade ** circuit

Farming, photographs, flowers, birds, social history, even alternative medicine: this circuit has them all.

From Miliou with its curative springs, walk south through well watered fields and orchards. The track verges are rich with seasonal flowers and birdlife. Climb out of a steep-sided gorge to explore the deserted hillside village of Theletra. Return with long views eastward to Mount Olympus and the Troodos mountains.

Generally easy underfoot, with some rough stretches. There is plenty of shade, but winter walking can be muddy. For more information, read *Discover Laona* (CY£2.50) by Adrian Akers-Douglas who researched this walk.

Logistics
Start-point: Miliou.

8.1   Miliou - Theletra: 4kms/2$^{1/}$2mls/1$^{1/}$4hrs, up 175m/575ft.

8.2   Theletra - Miliou: 6.25kms/4mls/2hrs, down 175m/575ft.

Total: 10.5kms/6$^{1/}$2mls/3$^{1/}$2hrs, plus time in Theletra.

Finish: Miliou.

8.1 Miliou to Old Theletra
Start from Agii Anargyri hotel (alt. 175m/575ft).

Agii Anargyri hotel was once a monastery. Its water supply is drawn from nearby sulphur springs, said by some to be beneficial whether taken internally or applied externally.

With the hotel on the right, walk away from Miliou, uphill, going south for 225m. As the main road curves away to the left at Pole 6, leave it and keep straight on south along a concrete track for 100m. Fork right, still south, down an earth track with a gorge below to the right. Look ahead between the walls of the gorge to see Theletra clinging on to its hillside.

The track passes through orange groves and bears right over a stream at a hut. Stay on the major track, forking left and curving counter-clockwise until resuming the southward direction. Rocks in the track glisten with crystal.

350m after the hut, reach a sign: ΑΠΑΓΟΡΕΥΜΕΝΗ ΠΕΡΙΟΧΗ ΚΥΝΗΓΙΟΥ = Game Reserve. No Hunting. Leave the major track which turns right: continue straight ahead, southward, uphill. The track levels out and the country opens up with Giolou *(Yoo-loo)* village across the fields to the left.
[1.25kms/³/₄ml/20mins]

Wind past orchard trees for 250m and fork right, uphill, going south. Descend towards a track junction after another 250m and keep descending left, south, into Neradhes Gorge, down to the stream-bed (alt. 350m/1150ft).
[1.5kms/1ml/¹/₂hr]

Still heading south, ascend past a hut by a pool on the right among orange groves. Birds like this quiet, fertile valley; bluebells flank the verges in spring. Fork left uphill, staying on the main track as it curves clockwise. Zig-zag steeply up to old Theletra village (alt. 350m/1150ft).
[1.25kms/³/₄ml/20mins]

Turn left down the concreted village street to explore.

The houses of Theletra cling to the mountainside like house martin

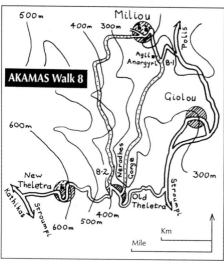

nests. Settled first by shepherds seeking summer pastures, the village dates back at least four centuries. Local embroidery was well known. The church (1755) has a fine carved screen from an earlier building and dolphin decoration.

Fearing landslip, the population of some hundreds moved out in the 1980s to a new village higher up the hill. Their old dwellings remain, gradually collapsing. A water-point still runs, just below the original (now dry) source in decorated stone.

8.2 Old Theletra to Miliou

Follow the village street uphill, out of Theletra. 30m past the last house, leave the concrete surface which turns left at a No Hunting sign. Take the lower earth track down to the right, along the edge of a gorge. The track ascends, northward at first, then eastward after curving clockwise round a re-entrant. After a stretch of concrete surface, ignore a fork up to the left: stay on the lower road, curving left past a No Hunting sign. The gorge is still below to the right.

Stay on the main track, ascending to the skyline past a limestone outcrop to the right. As the track curves left to go north, views open out over Giolou in the middle distance to the right, to the Troodos on the skyline. In March, huge orchids cover the verges. Reach a track junction.
[1.7kms/1ml/³/₄hr]

Ignore a track hairpinning back to the right. 15m after this, fork left off the main track to go north-west. Ignore lesser side-turns. Descend, zig-zagging steeply down a gravelly track into a gully and then up out of it to a 5-track junction at the top.
[1km/¹/₂ml/¹/₄hr]

Descend the second track on the left, northward past a hut [250m]. Take two right forks and then zig-zag down a rutted surface. As the road levels out, Miliou is visible on the left, to the north-east. Hairpin counter-clockwise with the major track, northward down towards Miliou for 250m: stay on the major, upper track, forking left. Go north into a clockwise re-entrant where tall slender cypresses grow out of a steep gorge to the right. The village is down a concrete track, with a crossroads at a telephone kiosk, water-point and taverna (alt. 200m/650ft).
[2.5kms/1¹/₂mls/³/₄hr]

Stay on the road, down to the south-east, past a florally overgrown dry water-point, out of the village, into orange groves in the valley below. Cross two bridges and reach the Ayii Anargyri hotel.
[1km/¹/₂ml/¹/₄hr]

Pafos Routes

THE PAFOS HILLS

This west end of the island was always quiet, the furthest from any development. Turks had grazed flocks here for centuries. Since the 1974 war, their abandoned hill-villages crumble away quietly, the better houses marked by decorative wrought-iron window grilles.

From the coast at Pafos, open country rises north toward the Akamas peninsula and north-east towards the cedar forests of Stavros. It's a region of bare, stony ridges, with vineyards and fruit trees in the valleys. Farmers and hunters keep open the old earth roads. Transport is usually needed to the start and finish. In a few cases, local buses can be used.

PAFOS: WALK 1   Grade ** linear
Drouseia or Pano Arodes to Cape Drepanon

North of Pafos, the Laona plateau lies across the base of the Akamas peninsula. From that region, a route descends south-west through gorge-riven hillsides to Cape Drepanon, giving frequent panoramic sea-views.

Down at sea-level, the track passes the mouth of the Avgas Gorge, a narrow cleft between high cliffs. Exploring this offers an optional diversion - but it involves scrambling over large slippery boulders among thick undergrowth.

Otherwise, the going is easy, apart from a brief stony section in the Koufon gorge. There is no water; shade is intermittent. Look for orange tape-markers and yellow waymarks.

Logistics
Start-point: Drouseia. Those based in Pafos could start from Pano Arodes: 24kms/15mls/about ½hr drive from Pafos.

1.1   Drouseia - Pano Arodes: 3.5kms/2mls/1hr, down 40m/ 130ft.

1.2   Pano Arodes - Anogia: 4.25kms/2$^{1/}$2mls/1$^{1/}$4hrs, descending 140m/460ft.

1.3   Anogia - Stavros: 5.5kms/3$^{1/}$4mls/1$^{1/}$2hrs, down 370m/1215ft.

1.4   Stavros - Avgas Gorge: 2kms/1$^{1/}$4mls/35mins, down 40m/130ft.

1.5   Avgas Gorge - Agios Georgios: 2.8kms/1$^{3/}$4mls/1hr, down 40m/130ft.

Totals: *From Drouseia:* 20kms/12$^{1/}$2mls/6$^{3/}$4hrs, plus time in Avgas Gorge, down 630m/2070ft to sea-level.

From Pano Arodes: 17kms/10$^{1/}$2mls/6hrs, plus time in Avgas Gorge, descending 590m/1935ft to sea-level.

Finish: Cape Drepanon: return by taxi: 24kms/15mls to Drouseia; 18kms/11$^{1/}$4mls to Pafos. A cafe in Agios Georgios would ring for a taxi - but it would be safer to book one in advance for an agreed price.

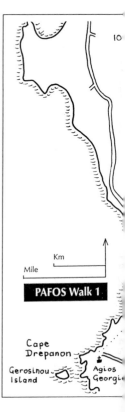

EITHER 1.1.1 From Drouseia

Walk uphill with the church and Supermarket Angela on the right. Fork left, east-south-east, at Christos' Tavern. Follow the Hospital road sign past the Health Centre and a little school to the southern edge of the village, where the tarmac runs out [800m]. The route crosses a stony plateau, cut into stone-walled fields. After 50m, continue over an earth crossroads, generally south for 1.5kms/1ml/20mins. Pass Pole 91-66 and turn right at the next earth crossroads, south-west into the northern edge of Kato Arodes, an almost deserted ex-Turkish village. [2.5kms/1$^{1/}$2mls/40mins]

At the metalled road, turn left and walk southward out of the village to Pole 76. Leave the main road and go straight ahead, with water-point ER 1954 on the left, south-east on a minor road. Pass a Moslem cemetery in a spinney to the right. Follow the power-lines into Pano Arodes and turn right at Pole 46.
[1km/¹/₂ml/10mins]

OR **1.1.2 From Pano Arodes**
Walk downhill, south-west through the village (alt. 590m/1935ft) with the church (and WCs) on the right. Pass Pole 46. Cottages, fig

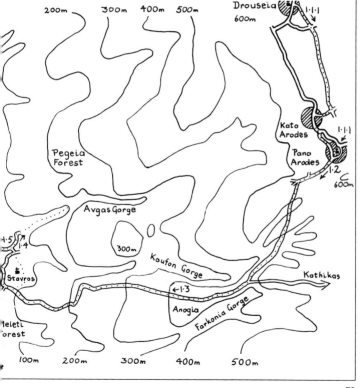

trees and stone walls peter out.
[500m]

1.2 Pano Arodes to Anogia plateau

At a derelict stone shed on the southern edge of Pano Arodes, fork right down a concrete road curving clockwise round a re-entrant. An earth road from Kato Arodes comes in from the right. Drouseia TV mast is on the skyline beyond. From the Pano Arodes junction, it's 1km/$^{1/}$4hr to a triple fork in the earth road.

Go left, southward, down and across a small ravine with vines in the bottom. Ignoring the track to the right, climb out of the ravine to go straight ahead on the level, still southward. Ignore three tracks to the left. 1km/$^{1/}$4hr from the triple fork, take a left fork downhill on a chalky surface.

For 800m/15mins a stony road zig-zags down to the floor of the Koufon valley. Pass the ruin of a stone house to the right (with its old mule-trail still visible across the road, going south-west up a gully). Over the stream-bed, high cliffs on the left give morning shade. Beyond the widening gorge on the right, the cliff changes into a stretch of clay slopes eroded into grooves.
[3kms/2mls/1hr]

This clay was traditionally used on house roof-tops. Builders laid flat roofs of canes or reeds across timber beams, plastering them with a final coating of mud. Every autumn, people put little piles of clay across the roof. Rain melted it down and filled the cracks. The clay expanded as it dried, providing waterproofing and insulation.

On the left, a chalky road comes in from Kathikas.

The trail curves clearly ahead, ascending clockwise from south-west to west along a bare saddle. The Koufon valley is now below to the right. Ignore a red arrow pointing left, down into the Farkonia Gorge (the upper Aspros). Shortly after a ruined stone hut on the left, the road rises to the stony Anogia *(ann-oy-ya)* plateau (alt. 450m/1475ft). Field workers have a rough shelter below one of the scattered carob trees.
[1.25kms/$^{3/}$4ml/$^{1/}$4hr]

1.3 Anogia plateau to Stavros

Ahead, the trail descends westward towards the sea. Aleppo pines replace the carobs and the surface underfoot changes briefly from white to red and then back again to white. The coast is visible from Cape Drepanon northward to Lara peninsula. At a battered sign ΑΠΑΓΟΡΕΥΜΕΝΗ ΠΕΡΙΟΧΗ ΚΥΝΗΓΙΟΥ (Game Reserve. No Hunting.) a brief diversion right for 200m leads to a view deep into the Koufon gorge.
[1.2kms/³/₄ml/20mins]

Back at the sign, follow the main route downhill, past more stone huts, to Bollard 60.
[1.1kms/³/₄ml/20mins]

From the bollard, the rough earth road curves counter-clockwise from north to south. After 500m, a left bend gives a viewpoint ahead to Cape Drepanon before curving clockwise downhill. Continue west on a level, broad red earth road that splits and rejoins. Reach a left bend with Bollard 124 among the bushes.
[2kms/1¹/₄mls/¹/₂hr]

EITHER: The road hairpins round the bollard and keeps on down for 700m to meet a high wire fence. Follow the fence 500m to the right, northward, turning north-east to a cliff-edge farm (alt. 80m/260ft).
[1.3kms/³/₄ml/20mins]

OR: An interesting diversion leaves the road 400m after Bollard 124, picking a way to the right on an indistinct vehicle track past a tin hut and wire enclosure. Walk north for 500m on a network of tracks through scrub to a banana plantation. Alongside it, among carob trees, is the little church of Stavros (alt. 80m/260ft). From Stavros church, take the earth road along the west side of the banana plantation and then turn left to the cliff-edge farm.
[1.5kms/1ml/¹/₂hr]

1.4 Stavros to Avgas Gorge

With the farm on the left, descend the earth road north-east into a flat-bottomed cultivated valley. Ahead is the junction of two gorges: the Koufon gorge to the right and the Avgas to the left. Walk north

through a stream-bed and fork right. Continue on a well-used earth road that runs north-north-east for 750m/¹/₂ml to the mouth of the Avgas gorge.
[1.2kms/³/₄ml/20mins]

Exploring the gorge has its hazards and is a matter for personal choice. The track squeezes round and over great boulders as the gorge narrows and deepens dramatically. Water and clay make surfaces very slippery. Thick undergrowth and loose rocks provide a congenial habitat for snakes.
[Add time spent here to the total.]

On the subject of snakes, St Helena (the Russian Tsarina Helen) landed in Cyprus while carrying part of the True Cross from Jerusalem to Constantinople. One of her recommended ways of ridding the island of snakes and other vermin was to burn them out. This proved successful, except in this locality, where the undergrowth would not burn.

Return to the valley stream-bed.
[750m/¹/₂ml/¹/₄hr]

1.5 Avgas Gorge to Agios Georgios
An earth road to the right ascends south-west, passing below a cliff-top taverna and down again to reach the coast in 15mins. Turn left on a broad stony road, walking south for 750m to a steep-sided flat-bottomed ravine where the Aspros valley reaches the sea.
[1.5kms/1ml/¹/₂hr]

The road hairpins inland, but a stony track scrambles down, across, and steeply up the other side of the inlet to rejoin the road. Paths over the grass between road and foreshore lead in 500m/10mins to fenced plantations. Aim for the church dome and a roofed terrace on the cliff-top. Bear right along the fence into a cluster of buildings on Cape Drepanon. Most are cafes, centred on Agios Georgios church. Swim in the harbour.
[1.3kms/³/₄ml/¹/₂hr]

The whole of Cape Drepanon was a Roman city. There are neolithic and Roman remains on Gerosinou island. Quarried tombs pierce low cliffs above the harbour. The ruins of a basilica date back to the 6th century.

PAFOS: WALK 2   Grade * linear
Kisonerga - Coral Bay

The growing village of Kisonerga (*kiss-on-ya*) is just north-west of
Pafos. Walk out from it on earth roads through orange and banana
groves, over a small plateau, across a gorge and up to the
Mavrokolympos (*mavro-koh-lim-poss*) dam.

A quiet road leads down a bare hillside with sea-views to the
coast. Then it's 10mins up a busy road to Coral Bay. This is a popular
resort with plenty of cafes and food shops as well as good swimming.

The half-day walk is easy underfoot but there's no water on the
way and not much shade.

Logistics

Start-point: Kisonerga, 8kms/5mls north-west of Pafos.

Total: 10kms/6¼mls/3¼hrs including stops. Ascend
110m/360ft; then descend 180m/600ft to sea-level.

Finish: Coral Bay, 11kms/6¾mls north-west of Pafos.

Transport: The Alepa public bus no. 3-7 leaves Pafos market at
0930hrs for Kisonerga: 25c for a 15min journey. Get
off at the football pitch. Frequent buses return from
Coral Bay beach or the Angela supermarket: no. 10
to the market, nos. 11, 15 to the harbour: 35c for a
30min journey. (*NB: Check current transport details on
the spot.*)

On the north side of Kisonerga sports pitch (alt. 70m/225ft), look for
a small school with a sign below to the Home for the Aged. Follow
the sign and fork right, passing the home and the neighbouring
cemetery all within 100m.

Stay with the main vehicle track. On the right, pass greenhouses
[350m] and a house with a shed full of fruit crates [600m]. The wide
stony track ascends north-north-east, parallel to power-lines and
then a ravine over on the left. On both sides are cabbage and
vegetable patches, among orchards and vineyards.

At a T-junction, take the left turn and walk straight ahead to the
north-west.
[1km/½ml/¼hr]

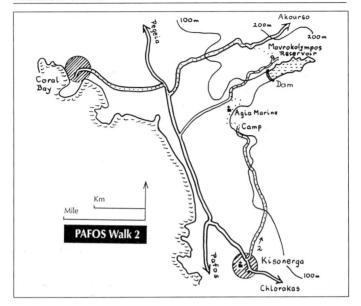

PAFOS Walk 2

A pomegranate hedge on the left is sometimes splashed with exploded scarlet fruit. Among the olives, lemons, avocados and oranges, watch for a sign forbidding photography. 300m after this, fork right between a line of conifers on the right and bananas on the left.

[1km/$^{1}/_{2}$ml/$^{1}/_{4}$hr]

Overlooked by a reservoir tank on a hillock to the right, the road passes between open fields, northward towards the hills. A rough gully cuts across the way and the road splits into a T-junction. Go right, following a tiny red arrow, to hairpin counter-clockwise round the depression and ascend north-west on to a stony plateau.

Bear left past a fenced camp for 250m/3mins towards the edge of the plateau. Between beehives to the right and a tree, go west down a rough track to join a stony road just below. Turn right on this, alongside a concrete drainage gully, shaded by the plateau scarp from the morning sun.

[1.25kms/$^{3}/_{4}$ml/20mins]

The road descends gently along the east side of the

Mavrokolympos valley, its bed green with orange groves. A tiny chapel stands just below the road edge. The valley was once a water-course, now dammed higher up to create a reservoir. After 10mins an iron gate and wire fence bar the earth road when it reaches the orchards. Zig-zag down left for 5mins along the fence to the valley bottom, opposite a stack of masonry ruins. Bird-watchers may spot black francolin down here.

[1km/$^{1}/_{2}$ml/$^{1}/_{4}$hr]

Turn left between the trees, away from the dam, for 300m and ascend right a few paces to a broad earth road. Follow this road up the west side of the gorge to the dam. Down below, an old stone bridge spans the vanished stream.

[1.5kms/1ml/$^{1}/_{2}$hr]

Keep on northward past the dam for 500m. Leave the main earth road and fork sharp left away from the reservoir, steeply up beyond the skyline to a metalled road (alt. 180m/600ft).

[1.25kms/$^{3}/_{4}$ml/25mins]

There's not much shade on the 2kms/1$^{1}/_{4}$ml/$^{3}/_{4}$hr descent down this road - just the occasional carob tree. A few ramshackle sheep-pens enclose patches of the stony open ground. Turn right up the busy coast road for 700m/10mins. Follow signs left into Coral Bay for a street of cafes, shops, banks.

[2.75kms/1$^{3}/_{4}$mls/50mins]

The sandy beach is 500m straight on down this street. It has WCs, beach bars, parasols, boats, no shade but plenty of people. On the way down, a dead-end sign on the left marks the way into a road with houses. Beyond them are steps down to a less used beach. To find a normally deserted shingle beach, take the earth road opposite the Golden Barrel restaurant. It has a little shade under the cliffs.

Bones found in caves near Coral Bay were long venerated as the remains of holy martyrs. They have now been identified as the remains of pygmy hippopotami. North-east of Coral Bay is Panagia tom Zalakion, the Church of the Varicose Veins. Sufferers traditionally go there to pray for a cure. Zulakia also means bramble, still used in homeopathy to treat varicose veins and rheumatism.

Walking back to Pafos isn't recommended. The first half is on the coast road through building developments. It's possible to reach the water's edge at Agios Georgios church and then to follow rocky tracks the rest of the way.

PAFOS: WALK 3
Grade ** linear
Letymvou to Marathounta via Stavros tis Minthas monastery

Touch four villages, a monastery and a golf course in this descending linear walk. After passing through closely cultivated fields and orchards, the route crosses an open landscape with long views over upland ridges. The final 4kms undulate along a quiet road through farmland with views south to the sea. End at a village cafe.

The walk is easy underfoot, but the second half has little shade. The monastery provides both shade and water.

The walk can be shortened by entering the route at different points: Kallepeia or Tsada.

Logistics

Start-point: Letymvou, Kallepeia or Tsada, all north-east of Pafos. For all three start-points, leave Pafos on the B7 road signed to Polis. Road distance to Letymvou: 16kms/ 10mls; to Kallepeia: 14kms/8¹/₂mls; to Tsada 10kms/ 6mls.

Totals: *From Letymvou:* 13.5kms/8¹/₂mls/4hrs, up 185m/ 600ft and down 200m/650ft.

From Kallepeia: 11.5kms/7mls/3¹/₂hrs, up 30m/100ft and down 200m/650ft.

An easier way from Kallepeia cuts off 1.5kms/1ml/ ³/₄hr.

From Tsada: 8.5kms/5¹/₄mls/2¹/₄hrs, down 290m/ 950ft.

Finish: Taxi from Marathounta, 8kms/5³/₄mls to Pafos.

3.1 Letymvou to Kallepeia

Descend Letymvou main street south-eastward from the church and war memorial (alt. 375m/1230ft) to a blue road sign for "Khoulou 7k".

Fork right up a narrow side-road going south-west. The road becomes a deeply rutted concrete track, descending steeply out of the village. Go straight down over a cross-tracks, along the flat valley bottom between oranges and almonds. Keep steadily downhill

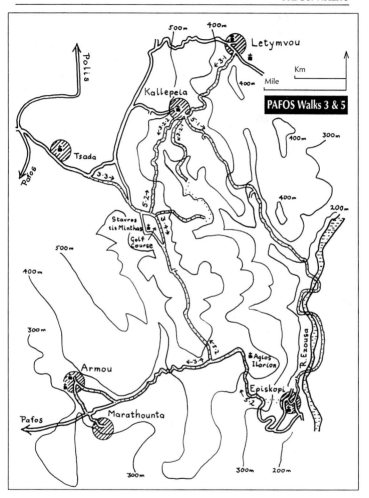

on the main track, under power-lines, past a breeze-block hut and iron gates. After 600m/10mins, the path starts to ascend. Zig-zag up westward for 150m and fork left over a concrete stretch. Curve clockwise up into Kallepeia past a bungalow with a white railing

81

and a FLORA tank on the roof to Pole 106 at a junction (alt. 490m/ 1600ft).

[1.7kms/1ml/^{1}/2hr]

    (The village church is 100m ahead, uphill past Clumber Lodge.)

3.2 Kallepeia to Stavros tis Minthas

Those starting the walk here should follow the first two paragraphs of Pafos Walk 5. Turn right at Pole 102.

    Walkers from Letymvou should turn left at Pole 102.

    Descend south-east past Pole 105, the cemetery on the right, a pair of big blue garage doors on the left, green gates on the right, to a track junction at the head of an open valley.

[600m]

Choose between two routes to Stavros tis Minthas.

EITHER: **3.2.1 Longer route** Go left from the track junction, contouring south-east along an earth road with terraces to the right across a valley. Fork left on concrete and descend a main earth road into a valley [350m]. At the bottom, the route bears left, parallel to another track on the further side of the valley bottom. It's muddy down here in wet weather.

[1km/^{1}/2ml/20mins]

    Keep south-east along the uncultivated valley for 500m, before ascending past a wire cage at the head of a little re-entrant. A ravine on the left is full of birds. The stony road forks right uphill for 500m and then again right uphill before petering out.

[1km/^{1}/2ml/20mins]

    A hunter's track continues along the edge of a gorge, below to the left. Push through thorny scrub and patches of old vineyard for 750m/^{1}/2ml. Watch for red paint and iron rods driven into the rock as markers. Follow these, keeping high and bearing right, to join a stony road. Turn right, uphill, for 200m and go left on a wide stone road running westward along a ridge. The earthworks on the skyline to the left are Tsada golf course. With the golf course on the left, walk counter-clockwise round its perimeter road to the monastery (alt. 520m/1700ft).

[2.5kms/1^{1}/2mls/^{3}/4hr]

OR **3.2.2 Direct route** Descend right from the track junction, past barking dogs in a compound, past a derelict blue Land Rover, counter-clockwise round a re-entrant and south-westward along the edge of Kallepeia into a terraced valley. Follow the main earth road across the valley bottom, rising southward to emerge at the head of a green basin, landscaped into Tsada golf course. Ahead and to the right, a clump of trees shelters Stavros tis Minthas monastery (alt. 520m/1700ft).

[3kms/2mls/³/₄hr]

3.3 Tsada to Stavros tis Minthas

Tsada villagers once made a business of collecting the aromatic small-leaved marjoram. It served as a culinary herb, a medicinal tonic, a massage oil, a disinfectant and a wood polish. White henbane also grows round Tsada. Although poisonous, it had herbal medicinal uses.

The Tsada start-point is 1km along the metalled road east-south-east from the village (shop, cafe; alt. 610m/2000ft), just after a pylon power-line, as the road bends left.

Follow the sign "Stavros Mythas Monastery 2k" east-south-east down an earth road through vineyards. After 1.3kms/20mins, reach a cross-tracks just before the golf course. Turn right to the monastery (alt. 520m/1700ft).

[2kms/1¹/₄mls/30mins]

3.4 Stavros tis Minthas Monastery to Marathounta

Access to the courtyard and small church is on the monastery's west side: shade, water, WC.

Gothic doors remain from the days when the bishops of Pafos used Stavros tis Minthas monastery as a residence. It is now empty apart from its black-robed, woolly-hatted custodian Barnabas. Hunters stay overnight in the autumn open season to make an early start. The buildings have been enveloped by a golf course.

From the monastery, pick a way across or round the golf course to its south-east corner near the golf club-house. Join a broad stony road running south with long views to the left across open country. Low yellow marker stones, inscribed "CYTA", mark the route. Fork left and continue south-east to a water tank and hut. Ignore the red arrow on "CYTA 8".

[1.5kms/1ml/20mins]

Take the right fork to keep south-east and ascend a ridge for 500m/10mins. The road then stays level for 500m, winding south and passing a fork to the right. Follow the major stony route as it curves down for 1km to the metalled Episkopi - Marathounta road, visible ahead. Reach it at stone "CYTA 11" (alt. 475m/1560ft).
[2kms/1¼mls/½hr]

Turn right on the road, going west-south-west through cultivated land. Donkeys graze in cropped fields; vineyards share stony terraces with orchards. Trees give some roadside shade. After 600m pass a marker "Mar 3" as the road zig-zags down. There are southward views before another zig-zag into a limestone ravine cut by the Kotehotis river.
[2kms/1¼ml/½hr]

It's another 1km/15mins south-west to a right fork, signposted to Armou village. Either continue 600m through hairpin bends along the main road or make a 1.75kms/1ml detour through Armou. The detour goes uphill between fields and then descends along the village street. Follow a "Paphos" sign south from a telephone kiosk back to rejoin the main road.
[2.75kms/1¾mls/¾hr]

Cross the main road southward, as signposted, into Marathounta village (alt. 320m/1050ft). After 250m, reach the Kebab Cafe, signed ΚΑΦΕΝΕΙΟ, a useful rendezvous for transport. The cafe owner has a small aviary of island birds behind the house.

Marathounta is the start-point for Pafos Walk 4.

PAFOS: WALK 4   Grade * linear
Marathounta to Pafos via Geroskipou

Almost the whole of this walk is visible from the start-point in a hillside village north-east of Pafos. Walk south towards the sea through a quiet fertile valley, with birds and spring flowers, into a canyon of clay and stone. Follow a road into a bustling village with cafes, shops, local craft industries, a fine folk museum and an unusual Byzantine church.

Continue through flat fields, vineyards and orange groves to a bar by the sea. A coast walk returns to Pafos.

The route is easy underfoot. Shade is limited on the first section and along the coast.

Logistics

Start-point: Marathounta, 8kms/5mls by road north-east from Pafos.

4.1: Marathounta - Geroskipou: 7kms/4¹/₂mls/2hrs, down 255m/840ft.

4.2: Geroskipou - Pafos: 8.5kms/5¹/₄mls/2hrs, down 65m/220ft.

Total: 15.5kms/9¹/₂mls/4hrs plus time in Geroskipou.

Transport: Alepa public bus No. 9 runs to Marathounta from Pafos Karavella bus station at 0745 and 1100hrs, Monday to Saturday: 25c/20mins for the 8kms/5ml journey.

From Geroskipou, Alepa bus No. 1, 2 returns to Pafos market bus terminus at 1400, 1540, 1610, 1635hrs on Monday - Friday. Last bus on Saturday leaves at 1130.

From Zenon Gardens, No. 11 bus runs daily to Pafos market. *(NB: Always check current transport details on the spot.)*

4.1 Marathounta - Geroskipou

From the Pafos-Episkopi road, follow the "Marathounda" sign south for 250m down past the Kebab Cafe ΚΑΦΕΝΕΙΟ (alt. 320m/1050ft). Continue for another 275m to Pole 56 on the right.

Take a concrete track down to the right, past Pole 56B, off the concrete and down by the cemetery. Descend into a wide valley, with the sea visible far ahead. After 600m, a concrete track joins from the left at an ER1959 water-point. Birds fly from an old dovecot among stone huts. Keep straight on down a concrete stretch for 40m and fork right towards a skyline mast. The rough road zig-zags down a little defile and levels out going south between vegetable patches. Reach a rough gully on the left.
[1.5kms/1ml/20mins]

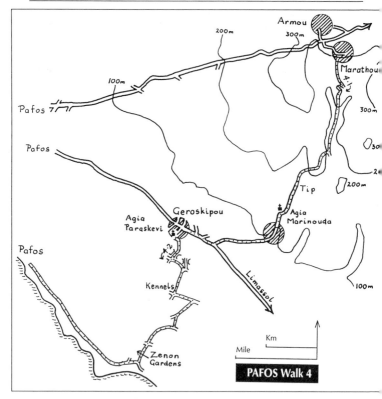

PAFOS Walk 4

Follow the road along the western edge of the gully which deepens into a gorge of rough rock and earthy rubble, enlivened by birdsong. Join a track along the bed of the gorge to a corrugated iron shed and wire-netting enclosure. Fork right, uphill out of the gorge, past a goat-pen.

[2kms/1¼mls/35mins]

The smell of the goats mingles with that of the town tip as the road bears right over a crest towards industrial sheds on the skyline and reaches a metalled road-end. Descend the road southward for 500m to Agia Marinouda church (water tap). 300m further on, fork right at a roadside water-point between Hadsons Cottage and a telephone kiosk. The road runs down alongside a stream-bed to the main Pafos - Limassol road. Turn right, west, for 500m up into Geroskipou *(Yeros-kee-poo)* (alt. 65m/220ft): cafes and shops. [3kms/2mls/1hr]

Geroskipou was first named Hieroskipos, the Sacred Garden. Devotees of Aphrodite paused among its trees and flowers on the way to their temple at Palaia Pafos. The village centres on Agia Paraskevi, a 5-domed Byzantine church with a 12th century Virgin, 14th century murals and a 15th century two-sided icon. 9th century paintings line the central dome. Paraskevi was a martyred Roman convert to Christianity.

Nearby, the Museum of Folk Art is well worth its 50c admission. Each room of an 18th century house is furnished or equipped to illustrate a different activity or trade. Allow an hour to enjoy it. Open Monday - Saturday to 1415, Thursday to 1745, closed Sunday. Closed Saturday in winter. Tel. (06) 240216.

Local products include pottery, basketwork and loukoumi (Cyprus Delight). Until World War II, local mulberry trees supplied a silk industry.

4.2 Geroskipou - Pafos

Start at Katsonouris supermarket, near the west end of the church. Turn left at Pole 71, following the arrowed sign for Kortos Pottery. After 200m, turn left at Pole 163. Leave the houses at Pole 172A, descending left to a concreted watercourse. Follow the earth road along the bank, going south-east with the water on the left. Pass orange groves on the right and reach a bridge crossing the water at an angle. [1.4kms/1ml/20mins]

Turn right for 30m and go straight ahead over cross-tracks. From here, the route picks a way through a chequer-board of fields, vineyards and orange groves. Anyone with a compass can find paths zig-zagging south to the sea.

Walk 350m south with a line of cypresses on the left to a residential dog kennels. Turn left at the cross-tracks for 200m. At a water valve in the middle of a track-junction, go right, south-west, alongside a cypress hedge, olives and water valve H7. Turn left, south, for 50m and right again at water valve H15. Bear left out of the trees and keep south through open ground between vines and oranges. After valve H20, go straight over a cross-tracks, past a blue-gated orchard, to the sea at Zenon Gardens restaurant and campsite. [2kms/1¹/₄mls/¹/₂hr]

Turn right along the coastal earth road, westward for 600m to Ricco's Beach taverna. Continue to Pafos with the sea on the left hand, skirting hotels and the Sodap winery. The surface underfoot varies from hard earth to soft seaweed, rock and loose sand. [5kms/3mls/1hr]

PAFOS: WALK 5   Grade *** circuit
Kallepeia circuit via Episkopi and Stavros tis Minthas
See Pafos Walk 3 for map p81

There's a remarkable variety of terrain on this route. From a little hillside village, walk downhill through its vineyards. Pass through a deep gorge, emerging in a wide cultivated valley. In wet seasons, a river has to be forded here more than once. Follow the river-bed to Episkopi, a remote, simple village perched under a massive crag. Shade is intermittent.

Either meet transport there, or walk up a quiet road to ascend Pafos Walk 3 in reverse. Cross bare hillsides past a disused monastery enclosed by a golf course. This section has no shade. Return across a cultivated valley to the start-point.

Logistics

Start-point:	Kallepeia, 14kms/8¹/₂mls by road north-east of Pafos.
5.1	Kallepeia - Episkopi: 8kms/5mls/2¹/₂hrs, down 340m/1115ft.
	Road from Episkopi to Pafos: 16kms/10mls.
5.2	Episkopi - Stavros tis Minthas: 7kms/4¹/₂mls/ 2¹/₄hrs, up 410m/1345ft.
5.3	Stavros tis Minthas - Kallepeia: 3kms/2mls/³/₄hr, down 70m/230ft.
Total:	18kms/11mls/5¹/₂hrs.
Finish:	Kallepeia.

5.1 Kallepeia to Episkopi
Travelling from Pafos, follow the road sign into Kallepeia downhill
for 500m, taking the first fork left, down to the church (alt. 490m/
1610ft): car park.

Keep the long front of the church on the left and descend
eastward on a narrow road between high walls. Bear left, past
Clumber Lodge, to Pole 106 at a fork. (The route from Letymvou
comes in from the left fork.) Turn right, south-east.

250m/5mins from the church, ignore the concreted left fork:
keep straight forward on an earth road. 750m/10mins later, bear
right on a broad stony road between stone walled vineyards along
an open ridge. Occasional black-clad villagers work the fields. The
skylined earthwork up to the right is Tsada golf course. Ignore
turnings right.

After 1.25kms/³/₄ml/20mins, the track descends over concrete
and leaves the stone walls. A ravine opens up on the left of the track
which forks right downhill into it.

Walk south along the ravine floor with the stream-bed below to
the right. Ignore a stony road descending from the right. High above
it, on the west side of the gorge, is a line of beehives.
[2.5kms/1¹/₂mls/³/₄hr]

The gorge opens out into a wide valley. After 400m, fork right
downhill past a clump of shade, the first since entering the gorge.
Reach a ruined high stone wall on the right.
[2kms/1¹/₄mls/¹/₂hr]

*The masonry was an aqueduct carrying water to a water-wheel that
drove a flour mill.*

300m after the wall, fork right at a cross-tracks, going south
through more ruins and orange groves to the wide, usually shallow,
River Ezousa. Turn right along the river bank for 100m to a ford.
Avoid crossing by pushing through bushes along the edge of a field
with the water to the left. A ford eventually has to be negotiated, by
hopping over on stones or wading. Follow the river south, past
tamarisk trees, along a wide flat valley floor for 20mins to the final
ford, with stones to its left.
[2.5kms/1¹/₂mls/³/₄hr]

Episkopi is visible ahead, sheltered under the big crag at the end
of the valley. Keep southward on the level earth track, passing the

first concrete road up to the right. After 500m, turn right, up through almond and peach orchards into the village (alt. 150m/490ft) on a concrete track heading for the church.

The village is a maze of narrow concrete streets across a steep hillside. At Pole 101-1, make a sharp fork right, going uphill for 500m to a turning bay. A sharp fork left leads for 100m between buildings to a telephone kiosk opposite a cafe on the right.

Ascend right, past Pole 43 on the left. At a whitewashed wall, fork right, past Pole 21, up a rough concrete road past water-point ER1953 to Pole 26. Just before a wrecked green Bedford bus, turn right, up to Pole 26-2.

[1km/^{1}/$_2$ml/^{1}/$_2$hr]

(The church (alt. 240m/790ft), with views of the Ezousa valley, is down the next road left past the wrecked Bedford. The main road is 500m further on, at a closed school, a bus shelter and Pole 40-1.)

5.2 Episkopi to Stavros tis Minthas

From Pole 26-2, a sunken mule-track ascends westward between walls. It's rocky underfoot and steep. Emerge at Pole PC 76, where power-lines cross the main road west from Episkopi.

[500m/^{1}/$_4$hr]

Turn right and ascend the metalled road, going west and then north. After 1.2kms/^{3}/$_4$ml/20mins, a sign "AΓ IΛAPIONA 200m" indicates a track right to Agios Ilarion, a tiny modern chapel. It's worth making the brief detour for views northward, all the way back up the Ezousa river valley. Resume the road which bends south-west, uphill for 800m. Cross the brow of a crest, just past road-ends to right and left. Turn off right at a low yellow marker stone on the right, signed "11 CYTA" (alt. 475m/1560ft).

[3kms/1 ^{3}/$_4$mls/1hr, including Agios Ilarion detour]

From the road, ascend westward, curving counter-clockwise up an earth road. Pass other yellow CYTA stones. At "9 CYTA", after 1km/^{1}/$_4$hr, fork right and continue on the major road. Ignore the red arrow on "CYTA 8" at a shed. This section crosses high bare ground (alt. 560m/1850ft), with long views eastward over rolling hills. Reach Tsada golf course and pick a way round or across it to Stavros tis Minthas monastery (alt. 520m/1700ft).

[3.25kms/2mls/1hr]

5.3 Stavros tis Minthas to Kallepeia

Walk uphill, northward, away from the monastery, towards a craggy knoll 500m away. Cross a broad access road and keep north, between the knoll on the left and a building on the right. Descend the main, creamy coloured earth road. Terraces rise to the left and views open out to the right. The big red roof of Kallepeia church is visible ahead across the cultivated valley. Reach the valley bottom. [1.5kms/1ml/20mins]

Undulate up from the valley bottom, along the southern edge of Kallepeia, past a derelict blue Land Rover, to a track junction. Turn up left, northward, past a pair of big blue double garage doors on the right, straight on up below a CORA roof water tank and solar panels, under power-lines, to a road junction at Pole 102. Fork left and go westward 100m to the church (alt. 490m/1610ft). [1.5kms/1ml/20mins]

Stavros Forest Route

STAVROS FOREST

Cedar-forested ranges surround Stavros tis Psokas (*stav-ross tis soh-kass*) alt. 780m/2560ft. The region never attracted settlers, apart from miners who felled trees to smelt copper from rich mines near Stavros.

The name is a corruption of Cross of the Measles, from the monastery and little church, closed in the 19th century. The valley spring, believed to ease the measles, never dries up. The river runs west and north to reach the sea in Chrysochou Bay at Polis.

Sought once as masts, the tall, straight Cypriot trees provided essential telegraph poles for the British Eighth Army in its World War II advance from Alamein to Tunis.

Since 1884, the Forestry Department has had a station at Stavros, managing the Pafos Forest District of western Cyprus. In its day, the British Colonial Department funded reforestation. Strict goat control has helped protect the landscape. Much of the Stavros forest was burned in 1974 during the Turkish invasion.

A cafe sells drinks and snacks; cooked meals or sandwiches need to be ordered a day in advance. Among the station buildings, a large Rest House hostel provides accommodation and meals for those who book ahead. Tel. (06) 332144 or 722338.

Access from Troodos and the east is via Kykkos, on broad earth roads carved across steep mountain faces. Tremendous views stretch across deep wooded valleys.

Coming from the west, leave the B7 Pafos - Polis road at Stroumpi. Allow 1¹/₂hrs from there to reach Stavros. After Pano Panagia, the forest roads are rough and remote from assistance.

Distances: Platres - Kykkos 37kms/22mls/1¹/₄hrs.
                    Kykkos - Stavros 27kms/16³/₄mls/1hr.
                    Pafos - Stavros 40kms/25mls/2hrs.

STAVROS: WALK 1
Mount Tripilos circuit

Grade *** circuit

Climb out of the Stavros valley on a woodland Nature Trail, over a col and on to a loggers' road. A steep path leaves the road for the top of Mount Tripilos. This is the third highest peak away from the Olympus massif and is easily accessible. Crests roll away to the horizon all round the summit. Return on the earth road and descend by a different Nature Trail, with long views almost all the way.

Look out for moufflon in a conservation enclosure, if not in the wild. Look and listen for warblers, as well as the martins and swallows at Stavros. Goshawks and Bonelli's eagles are said to fly above these forests.

Walking is easy underfoot, with no route-finding problems. The earth road provides views but little shade. Over one section, timber lorries can stir up dust, especially in the afternoon.

Logistics

Start-point: Stavros tis Psokas Forest Station.
Total: 23kms/14¼mls/7hrs, up and down 610m/2000ft.
Finish: Stavros.

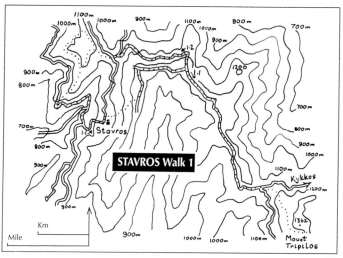

1.1 Stavros to Mt Tripilos summit

From Stavros Forest Station (alt. 780m/2560ft), walk up the Kykkos earth road, going south past the Rest House access sign. The road passes a fenced-off church on the right, bends north and then east to the Chorteri Nature Trail arch on the right (alt. 950m/3100ft).
[1.3kms/^{3}/$_4$ml/25mins]

Ascend the Nature Trail, initially southward. After 150m, fork left and zig-zag easily upward, generally north-east with views of the Stavros valley. Reach a green seat at a col with an earth road running north-south (alt. 1075m/3530ft).
[2kms/1^1/$_4$mls/50mins]

Go left, steeply up the earth road, northward, towards a peak with a fire-watch post on top. With radio masts above to the left, curve clockwise down - and counter-clockwise up. After 1km/^{1}/$_4$hr, go right at a junction with a wider earth road. This goes east for 750m/10mins to meet a major earth road at a Nature Trail arch and the back of a No Entry sign (alt. 1175m/3850ft). This is the main route between Kykkos and Stavros.
[1.75kms/1ml/40mins]

Turn right and walk south-east along a ridge. The wide earth road rises and falls, sometimes through cuttings, mostly through woods, often with views. Pass a stone hut on the right, ignoring the No Entry fork descending beside it. 500m/10mins later, reach a 3-way road junction marked Dodeka Anemi, with signpost and Forest Telephone (alt. 1100m/3610ft).
[3kms/2mls/^{3}/$_4$hr]

The track to the top of Mount Tripilos bisects the major earth roads and ascends east-south-east. Just past the Tripilos summit (alt. 1362m/4567ft) is a fire-watch post and a shaded picnic site (alt. 1400m/4600ft).
[2.7kms/1^3/$_4$mls/^{3}/$_4$hr]

Among the all-round views, Throni is to the east. The road from the fire-post continues southward down into Cedar valley.

1.2 Summit to Stavros

Return the same way, along the earth road to the Nature Trail arch and No Entry sign.
[5.5kms/3^1/$_2$mls/1^1/$_2$hrs]

Keep straight ahead on this main route northward towards Stavros. After 400m, pass a water-point on the right. It has good north-easterly views, but not always water. Follow the road westward, curving left downhill to a triple road junction with a green seat and Nature Trail arch (alt. 1025m/3360ft). A road sign indicates "Stavros 3k" to the left.
[2.5kms/1$^{1/}$2mls/$^{3/}$4hr]

Ignoring various white arrows, follow the Nature Trail arrow up some steps. Ascend westward on an easy clear path, to a bench at a counter-clockwise hairpin.

The trail splits here.

EITHER: Fork left to complete the hairpin and ascend 750m/$^{1/}$2ml/ 10mins to a north-south ridge. At the "Reforestation" sign, turn left to walk southward along the ridge. Ignore a yellow arrow to the right, indicating the other end of the alternative trail.

OR: Fork right and make a counter-clockwise sweep round the wooded hillside. Go left at all forks and stay high. This route, the Moutti tou Stavrou Trail, adds 1km/20mins to the total. Rejoin the shorter route on the north-south ridge. Turn right to walk southward.

There are seats at intervals, woods to the left and views to the right, over areas burned during the Turkish invasion in 1974. The ridge descends south on a rough zig-zag path to an earth road with a green sign "Lyssus 19; Polis 32; Zacharou 5", opposite a helicopter pad.
[Shorter route: 2.5kms/1$^{1/}$2mls/40mins]

Various rock-roses border the ridge path. The gum exuded from their aromatic leaves was once exported for use in perfumes and medicine. Collectors combed it from the beards of grazing goats.

Go left on the earth road, descending eastward to the Forest Station. A path to the left loops steeply round the moufflon enclosure.
[1.5kms/1ml/$^{1/}$2hr]

The moufflon mountain sheep (ovis ophion) once roamed these forests in large numbers. Very timid and agile, they were hunted almost to extinction. One king kept a pack of leopards for the chase. Now protected, moufflon can be spotted on the mountainsides. The herd kept in the Stavros enclosure helps survival. Lambs are born in May. Cyprus has adopted the moufflon as a national symbol.

Mount Olympus Routes

MOUNT OLYMPUS REGION
At the base of Mount Olympus, Troodos is the highest inhabited location in Cyprus, attracting walkers and winter skiers as well as day-trippers. Restaurants and market stalls, with phone boxes and a taxi, line a short street. The only food shop is Fereo's supermarket, open for the summer from 1 June. There is also a fruit stall. Cypriot, British and UN forces share the original British Army camp.

Walks from Troodos cross the Olympus massif, through forests and on mountainsides. There are frequent sweeping views across the island.

On the steep southern slopes of Mount Olympus, Platres first served as a hill resort for British government officials who found Nicosia too hot in the summer. The old Governor's cottage is now the President's residence. The British Army also developed Platres as a convalescent and recuperation centre. Their army chapel is now the police station. In World War II, the Forest Park Hotel served as a military hospital.

Still popular as a cool and quiet resort, the village has restaurants, shops and banks, as well as a daily bus to Limassol. Contact Charles in the square for taxi or minibus, tel. 421777 or 421220.

Grouped under the "Mount Olympus" heading, various linear routes are described between Troodos and Platres. These can be linked and reversed to make circuits. Walks south from Platres descend through broken country, scrub or woodland into a richer limestone landscape. This is the Krassachoria region, where vineyards lie between old villages, some still producing their own wines. Springtime flowers grow well here.

Further north in the Troodos mountains, springtime walkers enjoy famous displays of orchard blossom in the fertile valleys of Marathasa and Solea. These walks have the "Troodos" heading.

The Kaledonia Trail between Platres and Troodos

Trooditissa monastery courtyard
Pedoulas village, approached from Prodromos

Troodos Altitudes
(Different authorities give different heights.)

cf. Ben Nevis 1343m/4406ft

Agros 1010m/3300ft	
Foini/Phini 900m/3000ft	
Kakopetria 670m/2200ft	
Koilani 825m/2700ft	
Kykkos....................................1300m/4300ft	
Mandria..................................850m/2790ft	
Makrya Kontarka..................1680m/5500ft	
Mesa Potamos 1000m/3300ft	
Moniatis 730m/2400ft	
Mt. Adhelfi 1613m/5292ft	
Mt. Olympus 1952m/6406ft	
Mt. Papoutsa 1554m/5098ft	
Mt. Tripilos 1362m/4567ft	
Moutoullas 780m/2560ft	
Omodos...................................800m/2600ft	
Pedoulas 1090m/3580ft	
Pera Pedi 760m/2500ft	
Prodromos 1390m/4560ft	
Platres 1230m/4035ft	
Trooditissa 1300m/4265ft	
Throni 1318m/4324ft	
Troodos 1850m/6000ft	

OLYMPUS: WALK 1   Grade **/*** circuits
Round Mount Olympus

Known to Cypriots as Chionistra (snow-capped), Mount Olympus is the highest point of the island. A fenced radar globe prevents access to the topmost tip (1952m/6404ft), but there are panoramic views from the rest of its flat, rather scruffy, summit.

Two Nature Trails, Atalante and Artemis, ring the mountain at different heights, providing constantly changing views. A good day's walk covers both, in opposite directions, as well as reaching the peak.

97

The ascent from Troodos is stony underfoot and through woodland. The trails give easy going with little height variation. The west side of the mountain is open, with good views but little shade. Snow covers the high ground in winter, sometimes blocking paths on the northern flank of the mountain until Easter. Carry the Nature Trail booklet for botanical and geological information.

Two routes are given for the descent to Troodos. A double circuit with the longer descent rates Grade ***.

Logistics

Start-point:	Troodos.
Totals:	Ascent from Troodos to the summit: 230m/750ft.
1.1	Atalante circuit: 10.5kms/6$^{1/2}$mls/3$^{1/2}$hrs.
1.2	Artemis circuit: 10kms/6mls/3hrs.
1.3	Double circuit: 14.5kms/9mls/4$^{3/4}$hrs.
1.4	Summit from Artemis Arch and return: 3kms/2mls/1hr.
1.5	Short descent: 2.75kms/1$^{3/4}$mls/$^{3/4}$hr.
1.6	Long descent: 8.25kms/5mls/2$^{1/2}$hrs.
1.7	Summit and shortest circuit: 8.5kms/5$^{1/4}$mls/3hrs + taxi.
Finish:	Troodos.

1.1 Atalante Trail (average altitude 1750m/5740ft)
At the upper, northern, end of Troodos (alt. 1850m/6000ft), just past the last open-air cafe, walk west through the Nature Trail arch signed "Chromion" (not the Tourist Pavilion arch). Follow it for 900m/$^{1/4}$hr round a hairpin. Ignore the wide rocky road ascending right past a blue waymark: keep ahead on the level narrow path past a small red dot.

After another $^{1/4}$hr, reach a multi-track junction with a viewpoint sign and a green seat. It is easy to go wrong here. Follow the yellow wooden arrow immediately behind the seat. After 2mins, pass Marker 25, a drinking fountain, seats and a 3km post. Continue south, curving clockwise round the mountain to reach the final arch at a metalled road junction.
[9kms/5$^{1/2}$mls/3hrs]

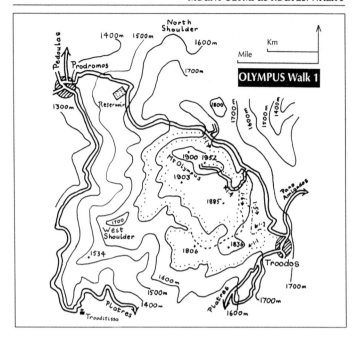

Turn right on the road to the nearby ski-lift. Walk 50m up the hillside below the lift cables and turn left on the clear Artemis Trail. Walk east-south-east to the metalled summit road opposite the Artemis Arch.
[1.5kms/1ml/¹/₂hr].

See later paragraphs for the summit and returns to Troodos.

1.2 Artemis Trail (average altitude 1850m/6070ft)
From Troodos, walk the first 900m/¹/₄hr of the Atalante Trail, hairpinning round a stream to a fork. Leave the level Atalante Trail and turn right past a blue waymark, ascending a rocky road south-west, curving clockwise until going north. At 1.7kms/1ml/¹/₂hr, reach a T-junction and go right, north, for 500m/10mins to join the Artemis Trail between Markers 5 and 6.
[3kms/2mls/1hr]

99

Follow the wooden arrow left, clockwise round the route as in the Nature Trail booklet. At Marker 17, on the south side of the mountain, keep the ski-lift and hut to the right while hairpinning left round a re-entrant. On the north side of Olympus, the trail passes under another ski-lift and ends on the road to the summit. The arch opposite marks the start of the Artemis Trail.
[6.5kms/4mls/2hrs]

See later paragraphs for the summit and returns to Troodos.

1.3 Double circuit
Walk the Atalante Trail as in 1.1 to its final arch.
[9kms/5$^{1/}$₂mls/3hrs]

Walk 50m up the hillside to the Artemis Trail. Turn right to follow it counter-clockwise round the mountain, giving different views. Reach the Artemis Nature Trail arch at a metalled road.
[5.5kms/3$^{1/}$₂mls/2hrs]

See later paragraphs for the summit and returns to Troodos.

1.4 Artemis Arch to Olympus summit
Walk up the metalled road, past the Cyprus Ski Club Cafe, 500m/10mins up the hill on the left. (WCs are inside the Exit door at the north-east corner of the building.) After another 250m/5mins uphill, take an earth road right, ascending through trees northward, curving to the west. Just past the top of the ski-lift is the dome perimeter fence: follow it left, south-west, to the main road and round right to the summit 1952m/6400ft. Return the same way to the Artemis Arch.
[Summit and back from Arch: 3kms/2mls/1hr]

1.5 Short descent to Troodos
Follow the Artemis Trail southward from the Arch for 500m/5mins to a wooden arrow and yellow paint marks. Don't follow the arrow, but turn left, south, down a broad earth road for 500m. Make another left turn downhill at an old yellow arrow on a tree trunk. Descend a rocky road, curving anti-clockwise from south to north and back to east. After 800m, rejoin the Atalante Trail. Turn left and hairpin back to Troodos.
[2.75kms/1$^{3/}$₄mls/$^{3/}$₄hr]

1.6 Long descent to Troodos

200m uphill from the Artemis Arch is an earth road signed "Pinus Nigras 350m". Follow it southward for 500m, keeping straight on past another earth road down to the left, past the Pinus Nigras tree, to cross the Artemis Trail at Marker 12 at a green seat and another yellow sign "Pinus Nigras".

Continue zig-zagging down the broad earth road into a valley of rough rocks and open pine woodland. After 500m, go straight over a staggered crossroads, south-west on the main track. A stream-bed to the right deepens into a ravine. Hairpin left into and out of a re-entrant and ascend to the right on to a ridge with views to the left down to the sea. Reach the end of the ridge.
[2.5kms/1¹/₂mls/³/₄hr]

Hairpin down right into a valley with a circular metal hut in its bed, beside a mine entrance. Other mine entrances dot the hillsides. Descend north-westward, past the hut, zig-zagging down the valley, which becomes a wide rocky ravine. Reach the Atalante Trail at Marker 38 and a yellow arrow.
[750m/10mins]

Turn left, north-west, against the arrow's direction, soon passing the 5km marker. Continue counter-clockwise along the trail to Troodos.
[5kms/3mls/1¹/₂hrs]

1.7 The shortest summit-and-circuit

Take transport to the top. Walk down, reversing 1.4. Follow the Artemis Trail as described, meeting prearranged transport at the Ski Cafe.
[8.5kms/5¹/₄mls/3hrs]

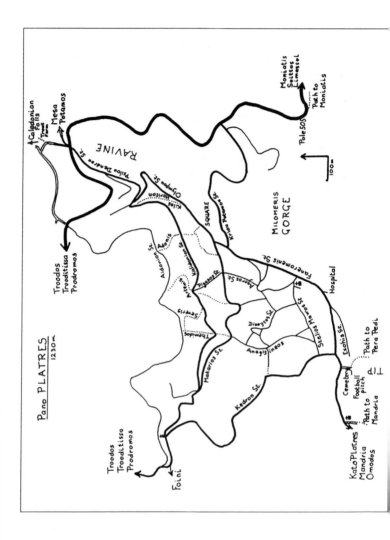

OLYMPUS: WALK 2   Grade ** linear
Troodos to Platres by Nature Trail

The Persephone and Kaledonia Nature Trails are clear and well engineered. They can be walked separately or linked into an attractive and easy downhill walk from Troodos to Platres.

Persephone is generally level and easy underfoot, leading southeast out of Troodos through open woodland to a splendid viewpoint. It returns the same way to the open-air cafes of Troodos.

Kaledonia leads southward, downhill to Platres. Shaded all the way by fine trees, the path crosses and re-crosses a pretty stream. Some sections go down log steps. The stream cascades over a cliff into the Caledonian Falls. Trail markers refer to descriptions in a free booklet "Nature Trails of the Troodos" available from Tourist Offices.

Logistics

Start-point: Troodos.

2.1   Persephone Trail: 6kms/3³/₄mls/2hrs.

2.2   Troodos to Platres on the Kaledonia Trail: 6kms/3³/₄mls/2hrs, descending 620m/2000ft.

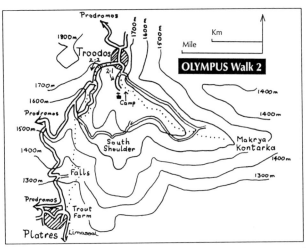

| ***Total:*** | 12kms/7¹/₂mls/4hrs. |
| ***Finish:*** | Platres. |

2.1 Persephone Trail

At the southern, downhill, end of Troodos, fork left, 300m uphill, past the Civic Restaurant and a green sign "Mesapotamos 13k" on the left to the police station on the right. Opposite the police station, turn left past a Nature Trail arch onto a clear narrow path.

With views to the left, the path curves along the hillside below the wire fence of a military camp. Follow the trail markers rather than any scattered paint marks. After the 2km marker, keep straight on south to Marker 21. Turn sharp left and begin a gradual descent. Walkers here have trodden a straight path across the zig-zags of the trail, but the general direction is eastward. A wooden litter bin and a "Viewpoint" signpost mark a cross-tracks with an earth road. (The earth road right figures in Olympus Walk 5.)

Follow the signpost, straight on between junipers and cedars of Lebanon, down to the rocky outcrop of Makrya Kontarka (*mak-ree-ah kon-tar-ka*) (alt. 1675m/5500ft).
[3kms/2mls/1hr]

Views stretch south across woods, vineyards and villages to Limassol harbour, salt lake and the sea. Close at hand is the greenish-grey outfall from Pano Amiandos asbestos mine.

A 17th century writer marvelled at Cypriot fabrics made of asbestos and even of asbestos paper which was passed through flame to erase the writing.

Return the same way to Troodos.
[3kms/2mls/50mins]

2.2 Kaledonia Trail

From the southern, downhill, end of Troodos, turn right and walk west down the Platres road for 300m. Opposite a sign to the Dolphin restaurant and Tourist Pavilion, take the road branching left among trees. This zig-zags steeply down through the "Seven Sisters" bends. Either just follow the road or cut across some of the bends.

Cut one off by following the power-line on the right away from the road, down a stony gully for 300m to rejoin the road at Marker F970 0-03. Pass the double green gates of the Presidential Cottage on the left.

The Cottage is private. Sometimes called a palace, it looks more like a Scottish Highland hunting lodge. A wall plaque notes that the French poet Rimbaud supervised its construction in 1880.

Turn left off the road at the right-hand gatepost, down a stony track across another bend. At the next power pole, turn off left again. Descend a path to rejoin the metalled road at a Nature Trail arch by a stone bridge over the Kryos Potamos river (alt. 1580m/5180ft).
[2kms/1$^{1}/_{4}$mls/$^{3}/_{4}$hr]

Between arch and bridge, descend the clear Nature Trail, following the stream through woodland to the Caledonian Falls. Some steep sections have log steps with hand-rails. Parts are slippery in wet weather.
[1.5kms/1ml/$^{1}/_{2}$hr]

This stream gives Platres a year-round water supply.

Stay on the path downhill from the green seat below the falls, following the stream for 1.5kms/$^{1}/_{2}$hr to the Psilon Dhendron (*pseelon den-tron*) trout farm and restaurant just above the main road. Across the road, go down Psilou Dendrou Street into Platres (alt. 1230m/4035ft).
[2.5kms/1$^{1}/_{2}$mls/$^{3}/_{4}$hr]

OLYMPUS: WALK 3
Troodos to Platres via Mesa Potamos   Grade *** linear

Round the south shoulder of the Olympus massif, an earth road makes a great dog-leg descent south-east and south-west. There are almost constant long views across the island to the sea.

Buried in the forests below the road is a disused monastery, accessible by a forest path or another earth road. Water is available at the monastery. The earth roads are easy underfoot, presenting no route-finding problems, but are largely unshaded. The forest path to the monastery has some steep gravelly sections, needing care.

Logistics
Start-point: Troodos.
Totals: Footpaths: 16.5kms/10$^{1}/_{4}$mls/5hrs, descending 850m/

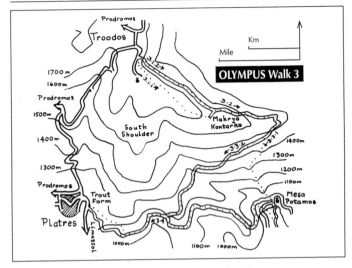

2790ft and ascending 230m/755ft.
Earth road: 19.5kms/12mls/6hrs, down 850m/2790ft
and up 230m/755ft.
Walking directly to Platres by earth road, omitting
the monastery extension, covers 11.5kms/7¼mls/
3½hrs and is an almost continuous descent, through
620m/2035ft, rating Grade **.

Finish: Platres: taxi from village square back to start-point.

3.1 Leaving Troodos
Start from Troodos police station (alt. 1850m/6000ft) as in Olympus
Walk 2. For this first section, choose between the Persephone Trail
and an earth road.

EITHER **3.1.1 Persephone Trail** Follow Olympus Walk 2.1. At the
viewpoint signpost just short of Makrya Kontarka, turn left and
descend northward to join the earth road route. Turn right.
[2.5kms/1½mls/¾hr]

OR **3.1.2 Earth road** Follow the green sign "Mesapotamos 13k"
along an earth road to a fork. The right fork comes down from the

Persephone Trail at Makrya Kontarka. Fork left downhill.
[1.75kms/1ml/¹/₂hr]

3.2 Round the mountain
From here on, look for yellow paint and orange tape-markers. The second stretch descends eastward on the broad earth road for 1.25kms/³/₄ml/25mins. The road then makes a sharp clockwise bend, passes through a short flat section and makes another sharp clockwise bend. The whole direction of the walk has now shifted south-west, giving extensive views across the island. The road has a steep drop to the left for 300m, until a wooded spur descends left, south-south-west, from the road.
[2.75kms/1³/₄ml/³/₄hr]

3.3 To Mesa Potamos *(messa pot-ah-moss)* monastery
Choose between a forest path and the earth road:

EITHER 3.3.1 Forest path to Mesa Potamos
Descend the spur steeply south-south-west, crossing an earth road after 200m. Continue down a steep gravelly path with a ravine below on the left for 1km through trees and clearings. After another kilometre on an easier woodland track, reach an earth road (alt. 1075m/3520ft) with a green signpost "Platres 7; Amiantos 7; Saitas 6". Walk 250m down to Mesa Potamos monastery (alt. 1000m/3300ft).
[2.6kms/1¹/₂mls/³/₄hr]

Many earth roads meet at Mesa Potamos monastery, founded in the 14th century and rebuilt every two hundred years. Deep in the forest, it made a secure EOKA sanctuary for George Grivas. The buildings are now dilapidated and closed to the public, while awaiting renovation. A drinking fountain is accessible at the gate.

From the monastery gate, walk down the lowest earth road, south-south-west. After 800m round a series of S-bends with a wooded ravine on the right, reach Fire Hydrant H 39. Turn right up a path with a stream to the left and walk north to a waterfall. Take a zig-zag track to the right, scrambling steeply up to an earth road. Go left for 30m and pick a way up to another earth road almost opposite a picnic site with drinking water taps and barbecue sites.

It's a popular week-end spot for families.
[1.4kms/1ml/^{1}/₂hr]

A shorter way to reach the picnic site from the monastery is to walk 500m south-south-west up the road signed "Moniatis 6k".

Walk 200m north-west up through the picnic site, to a broad earth road. (It was signed "Platres 7k" from the monastery.) Turn left and ascend southward. Join the earth road route at a green signpost "Troodos 9k; Mesapotamos 4k; Platres 3k".
[3.75kms/2^1/₂mls/1^1/₄hrs]

OR 3.3.2 Earth road to Mesa Potamos

Continue downhill on the main earth road. Ignore left forks before crossing two dry stream-beds of the river Arkolakhania. At the next wide track-junction, keep left, downhill, southward. Reach an earth road junction with a green signpost "Troodos 9k; Mesapotamos 4k; Platres 3k".
[3.5kms/2^1/₄mls/1hr]

To visit the monastery from here, follow the Mesapotamos sign left downhill for 4kms to the monastery and 4kms uphill back.
[8kms/5mls/2^1/₂hrs]

3.4 To Platres

From the signpost, follow the "Platres 3k" sign downhill north-west on the main earth road to the Psilon Dhendron *(psee-lon den-tron)* restaurant.

To vary the earth road, ascend right, opposite concrete Pole 161, and follow a mule-trail, parallel to the main earth road, up through the forest. Descend from its second junction left to the restaurant.

Cross the main road and walk down Psilou Dendrou Street into Platres (alt. 1230m/4035ft).
[3.5kms/2^1/₄mls/1hr]

OLYMPUS: WALK 4   Grade ** linear
Troodos to Platres by mule-trail

This is a spectacular path, along an old mule-trail that winds down the south shoulder of the Olympus massif to the villages below. It clings to a steep hillside, sometimes a cliff, overlooking a deep ravine. As well as passing through striking scenery, it gives extensive views over the island to the sea.

The path is well engineered and easy underfoot.

Logistics

Start-point: Troodos.
Total: 9.5kms/6mls/2³/₄hrs, descending 620m/2035ft.
Finish: Platres.

4.1 Leaving Troodos

Start from the police station (alt. 1850m/6000ft) as for the Persephone Trail in Olympus Walk 2. Stay on the metalled road south for 500m, past an army camp to the closed Anglican Church of St John in the Forest on the right.

Opposite the church, descend south along the camp perimeter fence, through a rusty iron gate. After another rusty gate, reach a green and white pole on the left. Ignore the road left, which goes up to the Makrya Kontarka viewpoint. Just ahead, the earth road bends

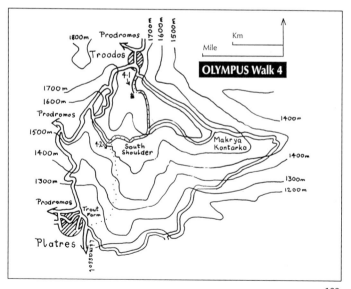

right between a brown seat and a very rusty finger-post.
[1.5kms/1ml/25mins]

Follow the rusty finger-post downhill to the west, reaching a green seat on the left.
[1km/¹/₂ml/¹/₄hr]

4.2 The mule-trail

Step down past the green seat and turn left, eastward, on a narrow path, once a mule-trail. After 300m, the trail turns south, gradually descending across a cliff-face and hairpinning in and out of three re-entrants. Look right, across a ravine, for views to Limassol and the sea.

At 1.5kms/1ml/¹/₂hr from the green seat, a path joins from high on the left. Look south-west to see Platres. The trail turns south-west away from the cliff and zig-zags down through trees. Just after a collapsed wall on the right, cross an earth road.
[3.5kms/2¹/₄mls/1hr]

Beyond the road, after 350m/5mins, fork down right for 400m to reach a white bollard. Fork right again, down to Psilon Dhendron (*psee-lon den-tron*) restaurant. Cross the road and continue down Psilou Dendrou Street 1km/¹/₄hr into Platres (alt. 1230m/4035ft).
[3.5kms/2¹/₄mls/1hr]

OLYMPUS: WALK 5   Grade *** linear/circuit
Platres to Troodos via the South Shoulder

Climbing northward out of Platres, this route goes up the Kaledonia Trail. It then winds eastward across the wooded South Shoulder of Olympus, ascending to Makrya Kontarka and Troodos.

The Kaledonia Trail ascent has a few steep sections and can be slippery in wet weather. The South Shoulder stretch goes steadily uphill and is easy underfoot. The walk is well shaded and has no route-finding problems.

Links are suggested to make circuits of varying length back to Platres.

Logistics
Start-point: Platres.

Total:	12kms/7¹/₂mls/4hrs, ascending through 620m/ 2000ft.
Finish:	Troodos: taxi from upper end of street back to start-point.

5.1 Kaledonia Trail

Walk north-east out of Platres (alt. 1230m/4035ft) up Psilou Dendrou Street, over the main road to the Psilon Dhendron *(psee-lon den-tron)* restaurant.

[1.5kms/1ml/¹/₂hr]

Follow the green signpost "Kallidonia 3k" up a concrete track past the Trout Farm on the right. Keep straight on up a few steps, past a concrete bollard. Follow the path uphill, generally north-eastward through woodland. Cross and re-cross the Yerokamina stream on stepping-stones. Reach the Caledonian Falls at Marker 38 (alt. 1300m/4265ft).

[1.5kms/1ml/¹/₂hr]

Take the well-trodden path away from the uphill side of the falls, southward, for 20m. The trail ascends log steps and follows the

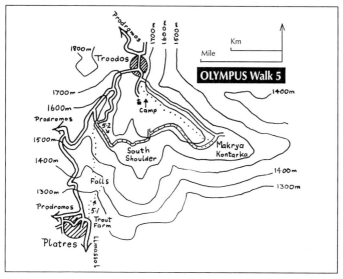

111

stream up a path with more log steps up occasional steep sections. It ends at a Nature Trail arch on a metalled road hairpin by a stone bridge over the Kryos Potamos river (alt. 1550m/5085ft).
[2kms/1¹/₄mls/³/₄hr]

5.2 South Shoulder to Troodos

From the arch, hairpin back right on an earth road above and parallel to the Nature Trail. After 750m, fork left up the major earth road past a green seat on the right.

(The green seat is the start of the mule-trail descent to Platres described in Olympus Walk 4.2. Following it from here makes a circuit of 12kms/7¹/₂mls/3³/₄hrs.)

The earth road rises through pine woods, curving left and right round the rocky hillside with views southward to the right. As the trees become sparser, the main track bends sharply left between a rusty iron finger-post and a brown seat. Ignore the footpath down right.
[2kms/1¹/₄mls/40mins]

150m past the seat, fork right at a green and white pole.

(The left fork at the green and white pole leads past the military camp to Troodos in 1.5kms/1ml/25mins.)

Walk east past blue paint marks on a level contour. Continue to the Makrya Kontarka viewpoint signpost.
[2kms/1¹/₄mls/40mins]

(A link here with Olympus Walk 3 makes a circuit back to Platres. Available options total 18kms/11mls or 26kms/16mls.)

Turn left and follow the markers of the Persephone Trail in reverse. The trail emerges onto the road at the police station. Turn right for 300m into Troodos (alt. 1850m/6000ft).
[3kms/2mls/50mins]

OLYMPUS: WALK 6   Grade *** linear/circuit
Platres to Omodos via Pera Pedi and Mandria

Look southward from Platres square to see the terrain of this walk. Below the square, woods slope steeply down to farmland and vineyards. Beyond them rises a low east-west escarpment and then

Hilltop church of Profitis Elias, near Moutoullas
Mount Papoutsa summit, near Agros

Right:
Water-point
near Troodos

Below:
Donkeys are
widely used as
working transport

a twin peak, Moutti tou Afami (alt. 1153m/3780ft). Omodos is behind the hills to the right.

The walk leaves Platres on a hunters' track down to those vineyards. On earth roads, it skirts the foot of the escarpment, passing through the villages of Pera Pedi and Mandria.

One option returns up the hill, making a circuit back to Platres. The linear walk continues south over the chalk escarpment and down through vineyards with views ahead to Omodos, understandably a tourist attraction.

Look for orange marker-tapes.

Logistics

Start-point:	Platres.
6.1	Platres - Pera Pedi: 6kms/3³/₄mls/1³/₄hrs, down 470m/1540ft.
6.2	Pera Pedi - Mandria: 4.25kms/2¹/₂mls/1¹/₄hrs, up 90m/295ft.
6.3.1	Mandria - Platres: 4kms/2¹/₂mls/1¹/₂hrs, up 380m/ 1250ft.
6.3.2	Mandria - Omodos: 6kms/3³/₄mls/2¹/₂hrs, up 100m/ 330ft, down 200m/655ft, up 50m/165ft.
Totals:	Circuit to Platres 14.25kms/9mls/4¹/₂hrs.
	Platres to Omodos 16.25kms/10mls/5¹/₂hrs. Allow an hour to explore.
Finish:	Platres; or Omodos and a 20min taxi drive back.

6.1 Platres to Pera Pedi

From Platres square (alt. 1230m/4035ft) walk south-west past the Splendid Hotel, down Faneromenis Street, passing church, school and hospital. Follow the Stadium sign along Exohis Street and turn left in front of the walled cemetery to an ungrassed football pitch. [1km/¹/₂ml/¹/₄hr]

To the left, just after Pole 292-7, descend south-east on a hunters' path through lightly wooded slopes. The town tip rises to the right and a ravine falls away to the left. In 25mins reach a stone bridge, once on a mule-trail, now almost lost among the trees.

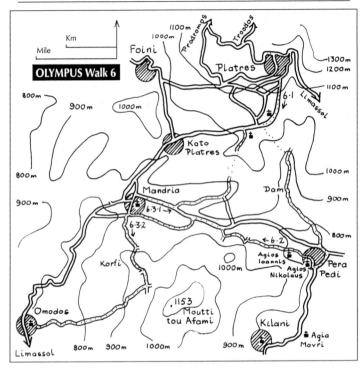

Follow the path over the bridge with the ravine and then a power-line on the right. Zig-zag round a little re-entrant and reach a broad earth road at Pole 78/TA82.

[1.5kms/1ml/$^1/_2$hr]

Bear right, southward, for 400m down the earth road, over a concrete reinforcement, to a little reservoir that serves Pera Pedi. Another 400m after that, fork left, past a farm on the right. Below the farm, the Chryospotamos valley widens out into cultivated fields, an almond orchard flanks the road and brambles reinforce the fence. Follow a power-line round a bend with a seat, past an inverted amphora, to the Pera Pedi - Mandria road where a green telephone kiosk stands between two cafes.

[2kms/1$^1/_4$mls/$^1/_2$hr]

This road is the northern limit of the Krassachoria wine region. Pera Pedi has been a farming community since the 16th century, growing good apples and productive vines. The Keo winery has been processing local grapes since 1891. Agios Nicolaus church (1796) has a 16th century icon of the Virgin Mary.

300m to the left along the road, another cafe and a mini-market flank a road junction. From the junction, follow the Koilani road-sign for 300m, turning off right opposite Pole 43 at a Co-op sign up a small road north-west into the village (alt. 760m/2500ft).

The Koilani road is also signed to the 15th century church of St Mavra. Fleeing a forced marriage, the pious Mavra hid in a cave. For her further protection, the Virgin Mary caused a stream to flow from the rocks. The stream is now a holy spring.

Walk up past a stone water-point and keep taking right turns for 200m to reach Agios Nikolaus church on the left (water tap). Follow a narrow street of deserted houses, with old whitewash on grey stone and faded blue paint still clinging to some of the old wooden doors. Past a clump of oleander, turn right at Pole 14 to the new Agios Ioannis church among trees (WC and tap.)
[1.5kms/1ml/$^{1}/_{2}$hr]

The pink-flowered, almond-scented oleander exudes a highly poisonous milky sap. People stuffed the twigs into mouse and rat holes so that vermin had to chew their way out.

6.2 Pera Pedi to Mandria

From the church, walk westward, between the escarpment to the left and the main road occasionally visible to the right. 300m past the church, among developing buildings, climb left up a short flight of concrete steps. Follow the power-line right, walking west-north-west for 1km/20mins along an earth road through old vineyards, past occasional new houses, to a T-junction.

Ascend left, then right, towards the west again, for 700m/15mins to an earth road junction. From there it's 100m right to a STOP sign on the metalled Mandria-Pera Pedi road. Above, a signals mast stands on the escarpment.
[2kms/1$^{1}/_{4}$mls/40mins]

Keeping westward, turn left along the metalled road for 400m, branching left again onto a parallel earth road. Passing a terraced hillock on the right, the broad, dusty trail moves in and out of the shade of olive and walnut trees with vineyards on both sides. As a power-line crosses overhead, the village of Mandria comes into view ahead.

1km after leaving the main road, take the centre track at a triple fork, curving downhill for 400m to the south-east edge of Mandria at Pole 14 (alt. 850m/2790ft). Turn right up the village street for 500m, past a water-point, to a shaded rest-place by the church, a telephone kiosk and a few shops.
[2.25kms/1¹/₂mls/40mins]

Choose between a circuit back to Platres or walking on to Omodos.

EITHER 6.3.1 Mandria to Platres
From Mandria church, walk up the hill and turn right at the road junction for Pera Pedi. After 800m, reach a blue and white shrine on the left, opposite Pole 88 at a fruit farm. Turn left at the shrine, north-east up an earth road for 200m. Fork right, still north-east, with vineyards and orchards in the valley below to the left, and right again, towards a red-roofed building on a knoll.

At a T-junction, turn left and walk north. Keep the red-roofed building on the left and curve counter-clockwise round it. Ascend northward through orchards for 500m/10mins. Leave the main track and go up a gravelly zig-zag ascent on the left.
[1.5kms/1ml/¹/₂hr]

Ascend generally north on a wide path between sandy hillsides dotted with trees. After 600m/12mins, the track becomes an earth road, bearing right between sandy hillocks and immediately descending left towards Platres on the hillside ahead. Keep straight on past a house on the left to Faneromini church and a shrine by the road.
[1km/¹/₂ml/20mins]

Turn right up the road into Platres (alt. 1230m/4000ft).
[1.25kms/³/₄ml/¹/₂hr]

OR 6.3.2 Mandria to Omodos
From Mandria (alt. 850m/2790ft) the direction is south-west. Return to Pole 14 and follow the metalled road out of the village. Just after

Pefkos Villa on the right, leave this route (which hairpins right) and continue ahead, south-westward, on an earth road between the Khapotami stream-bed on the right and power-lines on the left.

After 350m, at a cream and red villa on the right, take the left-hand uphill fork, curving counter-clockwise past a transformer pole TB 40 A. Fork left off the major earth road, ascending south-east, quite steeply upward, to join a major chalky road. Look back for views. Go right, still upward, across a crossroads, to the narrow Korfi pass (alt. 950m/3120ft).

[2kms/1¼mls/¾hr]

In front lies a valley of chalk-soiled vineyards, with just an occasional tree to give shade. Walk southward down from the pass for 300m to a T-junction. Turn left past a black and white No Hunting sign.

After 350m/10mins, turn right at the next T-junction and contour westward, with the red buildings of Omodos visible ahead on the facing hillside. Reach a crossroads with a green and white Game Reserve Area sign: turn right, downhill, to the south-west. Ignore all uphill forks. Pass a blue solid iron gate in a dry-stone wall on the left: 300m later, keep straight on westward for Omodos, ignoring a left turn.

Zig-zag steeply down to the Khapotami stream-bed (alt. 750m/2460ft) and 600m/¼hr up again into Omodos at Pole 9-M 93. Curve clockwise up through narrow alleys for 400m to the village centre (alt. 800m/2625ft).

[4kms/2½mls/1½hrs]

People settled on these southern slopes of the Troodos mountains, the Krassachoria, over eight centuries ago, growing fruit and vines.

The simple prettiness of Omodos attracts tourists. But behind the lace shops and honey stalls, it is still a working village with donkeys and work-yards. Unspoiled old houses line pastel-painted, flower-decked alleys. The ancient village wine press survives and has been carefully restored.

At the end of the square, the monastic church houses religious relics. A fragment of the True Cross is encased in glass and locked within a silver cross. It is inspected twice a year, on Easter Day and Holy Cross Day. Another silver cross holds shreds of the rope that bound Christ. A British officer's memorial plaque (1811) is on the outside wall. Nearby, the Museum of the Struggle records the EOKA uprising.

The annual fair is on 14 September.

OLYMPUS: WALK 7   Grade ** linear
Platres to Saittas crossroads

Just outside Platres, a hunters' track drops down from the main
road, going southward along a wooded ridge. From the end of the
ridge, the route descends over steep gravelly slopes, through sharp
scrub, with views through the trees to the farmland below. The
route levels out through vineyards and orchards to Moniatis, an
unspoiled hillside village. A footpath leads on, down through
pleasant woodland, to the crossroads outside Saittas, near Trimiklini
Dam.

Look for orange marker-tapes.

Logistics
Start-point: Platres.
Total: 8kms/5mls/2³/₄hrs, descending 630m/2070ft.
Finish: Saittas crossroads: taxi back.

7.1 Platres to Moniatis
From Platres square (alt. 1230m/4035ft), opposite the International
Cazino, descend Kriou Potamou Street. At 850m/10mins, follow a
road sign "Saittas 7; Limassol 38" south down the main Limassol
road. Just after a km-stone "B8 Mon 4 PPl 4" and a cutting, the road
turns left, northward. Stop at Pole 505.
[1.75kms/1ml/¹/₂hr]
     Descend some rough steps on the right and walk through tipped
rubbish up towards a wooded ridge about 50m ahead. Follow the
hunters' narrow track through trees along the ridge southward,
curving clockwise to south-east. Look left for views. The ridge ends
after 400m on a knoll called Yerajes.
     Descend left through bushes, going eastward down a spur on a
faint steep, gravelly path. Reach an open rocky patch with a view
down to Moniatis.
[1km/¹/₂ml/20mins]
     After another 600m descent, two plastic barrels and then a water
tank mark the start of irrigated terraces. Bear right, south-west, to an
earth road-head. Go left through an arch of vine poles and left again
at a T-junction on a wide earth road. Then zig-zag east to the main
118

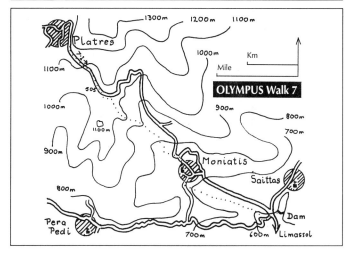

road at Pole TF 34.
[1.75kms/1ml/³/₄hr]

Descend the road right for 200m past a house, a black-and-white striped safety wall and a shrine. The first metalled road on the right leads south down into Moniatis (alt. 730m/2400ft). At the beginning of the village, take a narrow concrete path on the right, parallel to the road, past the church, post office and a shop to the village square with a phone box, a simple cafe and a water fountain. Moniatis has a Rural Taxi.
[500m/¹/₄ml/10mins]

7.2 Moniatis to Saittas

Walk downhill from Moniatis square towards the main road (where there are two cafes and a shop). Turn right after 300m, following a "Perapedhi 6k" sign. Continue for 500m, past the cemetery, where the metalled road surface ends, to Pole 29-14. Fork left downhill from the main earth road, past a right turn to a youth camp and a left turn to a goat-pen, curving clockwise and crossing a stream-bed after 200m.

Zig-zag along a path contouring clockwise round high ground for 130m: then fork up right from the broad track onto a narrow

119

path.

Follow this pleasant track through pinewoods east-south-east for 500m to another stream-bed. Continue clockwise round the high ground for 500m to a metalled road-head.

[2.25kms/1¹/₂mls/³/₄hr]

Walk downhill 100m to Pole 19 and fork left 300m past houses to the main road. Turn left, downhill for 300m to Saittas crossroads (alt. 600m/1970ft): shop, telephone kiosk, Swan's Lake Tavern and Trimiklini Dam.

[700m]

OLYMPUS: WALK 8   Grade *** circuit
Plattes circuit via Foini and Trooditissa

The circuit starts on a quiet road descending westward through orchards out of Platres into Foini village (pronounced *fee-nee* and spelt Phini on most maps). An earth road then goes northward up to Trooditissa Monastery, tucked into a niche high on the hillside. Two tracks continue up to the West Shoulder of the Olympus Range. There they rejoin to bear east and south-east, downhill back into Platres.

Most of the route is easy underfoot. The ascent is steep in places, with a few rough stretches. Shade is limited until reaching the tree-line at the monastery. Foini has cafes; there is water at Trooditissa *(troh-dee-tissa)*. There are frequent good views.

Logistics
Start-point: Platres.
Totals: *Longer route:* 22kms/13¹/₂mls/6³/₄hrs.
    Shorter route: 16kms/10mls/5hrs.
    Down 330m/1080ft, up 600m/1970ft, down 275m/ 900ft.
Finish: Platres.

8.1 Platres to Trooditissa
Walk west out of Platres (alt. 1230m/4035ft) on Kalidonion Street, past the Forest Park Hotel, following the road signs "Limassol 50k"

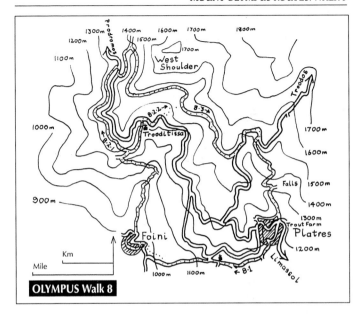

and "Trooditissa 5k" for 750m. At Pole 514, follow a "Phini" arrow left downhill for 2kms/1¼mls.

Reach a T-junction and turn right, down through a road-cutting. Or, at 1.5kms/1ml, cut off the corner and the cutting: as a house and signals mast come into view ahead, turn right down a little path, bearing left into a stony gully towards the metalled road below. Turn right and descend gradually to rejoin the road at a stone water-point dated 1909.

Walk downhill to a "Limassol 48k" sign and turn left off the road down into Foini village. After a Taxi sign and an ER 1955 water-point on the right, reach the Pivlakion Pottery Museum. Follow a "Phini Tavern" arrow along a curving street to shops, cafes and a war memorial (alt. 900m/3000ft).

[3.5kms/2½mls/1hr]

Using local clay, pottery was the original industry of Foini. An enthusiast, Mr Pivlakis, has collected examples of traditional pots in a village house and yard.

Trooditissa monastery entrance`

Bear right, uphill, past Pole 125 for 200m to a "Limassol 49k" sign. Leave the metalled road and walk up past two cafes, following a "Fresh Trout" arrow. Look left after 200m to see the remains of a stone aqueduct, once used to drive a mill-wheel. Ascend right at the next fork, passing the trout farm below to the left. Stay on the main track with the rock face on the right.

500m after the trout farm, fork left, slightly downhill, past a Greek sign XANTAPA in blue and ΚΑΘΑΡΟ in black, to curve counter-clockwise round a re-entrant with a waterfall. Continue uphill, with views opening out to the south and west over limestone valleys and farmland. Take right forks and reach a T-junction with a broad earth road.
[3kms/2mls/1hr]

Turn right, uphill. Note, but ignore, a turn off to the left on the way to Trooditissa Monastery (alt. 1300m/4265ft). WCs, cafe (occasionally open).
[1.5kms/1ml/¹/₂hr]

Visitors are required to dress appropriately: no bare shoulders or legs. The monastery is closed 1200-1400hrs.

Legend tells that in the 8th century AD, a pillar of fire led a monk here with an icon of the Virgin Mary, painted by St Luke. He hid the icon in a cave where it lay until revealed in 990 AD. The monastery was founded in 1250 as a shrine. Nine monks lived there to protect the icon. After the Turks destroyed the building in 1885, the icon was found buried under an apple tree in the garden. A copy of the icon hangs over the south door. A leather girdle hung with silver is said to remedy infertility in women. The two thrones are carved from walnut. Trooditissa is the highest monastery in Cyprus. An earlier name was Afroditissa.

Choose between two routes onward from the monastery:

EITHER 8.2.1 Longer hillside route
Return past the WC block and follow the green sign "Ayios Dimitrios 9k" downhill for 1km/20mins to the first turning up right - noted on the way up.

Turn right up the earth road. Go right at all forks. Continue for 2.6kms/1$^{1}/_{2}$mls/$^{3}/_{4}$hr to a metalled road (alt. 1350m/4430ft). [3.6kms/2$^{1}/_{4}$mls/1$^{1}/_{4}$hrs]

Walk right, uphill, for 50m to a road marker E804 9-02. Opposite this, follow the green sign "Prodhromos Dam 6k", hairpinning up left for 750m/15mins to join another earth road. Ignore the left turn (which goes to Prodromos).

Turn right and keep descending southward. Take a sharp left bend, ignoring the path straight ahead (which descends steeply back to the monastery).

Follow the broad earth road down, with views out to the right over the forested hillsides and the monastery. Hairpin clockwise into and out of the Xerokolymbou river re-entrant: at head level to tne left, the original mule-trail route is still visible. 500m/10mins after this, white paint and yellow tape-markers on the right indicate the junction with the shorter route up from the monastery. [3.25kms/2mls/1hr]

OR 8.2.2 Shorter route to Platres
Turn right out of the monastery and right again, along the main road, curving for 500m round a rocky headland, above steep wooded hillsides. Turn left up through a picnic site (water taps) for 300m. Behind a painted shrine on the right, follow a red arrow and yellow tape-markers up a mule-trail. Zig-zag north-east for 750m,

Donkey

past a mossy triangular bollard, to a wide earth road. This is the junction with the longer route up from the monastery. Turn right. [1.75kms/1ml/^{1}/$_{2}$hr]

8.3 Joint return to Platres
Make a gradual ascent generally south-east to the main Platres-Troodos road.
[1.75kms/1ml/^{1}/$_{2}$hr]

Walk left up the road for 700m, curving clockwise. Descend the first earth road down to the right past a brown wooden sign ΔΡΟΜΟΣ ΚΛΕΙΣΤΟΣ. After 2kms, ignore the left turn signed uphill to Caledonian Falls and keep on down through the woods for 1km to a bent green signpost. Turn right, curving clockwise on an earth road for 400m and forking left down to the main Platres-Troodos road at Pole 444.
[4.3kms/2^{1}/$_{2}$mls/1^{1}/$_{2}$hrs]

Cross the road and follow the blue sign to "Private Residences" - this is Aidonion Street. At Pole TE6-28, after 275m, turn left down a steep woodland footpath to Kalidonion Street in Platres (alt. 1230m/4035ft).
[500m]

Other Troodos Routes

This pleasant linear route curls southward round the western flank of the Olympus massif, with a choice of descents into Platres. One of these reverses Olympus Walk 8.1; the other joins the final stage of Olympus Walk 8.3.

The walking is on earth roads, easy underfoot, with fine views almost all the way.

Logistics

Start-point:	Prodromos, 14kms/8³/₄mls by road from Platres.
Total:	16kms/10mls/5hrs, up 160m/525ft, down 320m/1050ft.
Finish:	Platres.
	Taxis available in both villages.

1.1 Prodromos *(prod-roh-moss)* **reservoir**
Prodromos claims to be the highest village in Cyprus, on the grounds that Troodos is not a proper settlement. It also boasts the purest air and the best apples. Trikoukkia agriculture station and the national Forestry College are just outside the village. The big Berengaria Hotel closed in 1980. Prodromos means "predecessor" - John the Baptist.

Start at the north-east end of Prodromos (alt. 1390m/4560ft) at a 5-road junction with room to park. Opposite a supermarket and the Prodromos Restaurant is a telephone kiosk, a water tap and a shrine. WCs are just down a side-road signed to the Forestry College. Local taxi (1994): tel. 462041. Look for red/white tape-markers on this section.

Walk downhill 150m on the Pedoulas road to a "Slippery Road" sign. Turn right just after Pole 111 and walk up through a children's playground for 200m. Beyond three green/white metal posts, ascend

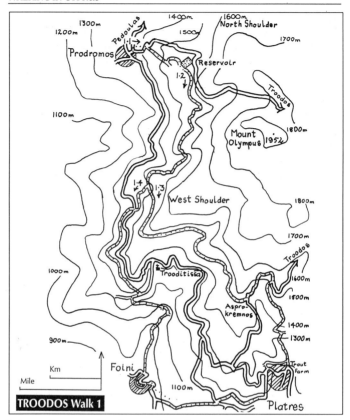

TROODOS Walk 1

left on the main Prodromos-Troodos road for 500m to a bend. Follow a green and white finger-post up an earth road right, signed "Dead End Road".

Views to the right over the valley to Prodromos open out from this section. Ascend south-east past Bollard 561. At Bollard 540 turn sharp left uphill, curving clockwise for 300m (some red waymarks) to Pole 23. From a track fork, ascend south-east past some wooden WC huts and a picnic area to the west corner of Prodromos reservoir (alt. 1550m/5085ft).

[2.4kms/1¹/₂mls/1hr]

126

1.2 Reservoir to Olympus West Shoulder

With the reservoir on the left, go counter-clockwise round its south corner, then right, east, through trees and past some green seats, nearly to the metalled Prodromos-Troodos road.

Stay on the earth road, bearing right, downhill to the south. 400m from the reservoir, pass Picnic/Camping and No Entry signs on the right.

Follow the broad earth road south with views north back to Prodromos and west to Kykkos and Throni. The earth road loops clockwise round four re-entrants below the Olympus West Shoulder. Ignore a right turn with an illegible metal sign: continue on the major earth road for 500m to a fork (alt. 1550m/5085ft) with waymarks of many colours.
[4kms/2$^{1/2}$mls/1hr]

Choose between descents of similar length via Asprokremnos or via Foini.

EITHER 1.3 Descent to Platres via Asprokremnos

Fork left (red/white tape-markers) and keep descending southward to a sharp left bend. Ignore the path going straight ahead (which leads steeply down to Trooditissa Monastery).
[1.25kms/$^{3/4}$ml/$^{1/2}$hr]

Stay on the main track, descending eastward out of woodland, with views out to the right over the forested hillsides to farmed lowlands. Look down to see Trooditissa Monastery. Hairpin clockwise into and out of the River Xerokolymbou re-entrant: at head level to the left, the original mule-trail route is still visible. Make a gradual ascent generally south-east to the main Platres-Troodos road at Asprokremnos.
[3.25kms/2mls/1hr]

Walk left up the road for 700m, curving clockwise. Descend the first earth road down to the right past a brown wooden sign ΔΡΟΜΟΣ ΚΛΕΙΣΤΟΣ. After 2kms, ignore the left turn signed uphill to Caledonian Falls and keep on down through the woods for 1km to a bent green signpost.

Turn left and walk down past the trout farm into Platres (alt. 1230m/4035ft).
[4.75kms/3mls/1$^{1/2}$hrs]

OR **1.4 Descent to Platres via Foini**

Take the right fork downhill, following white tapes and orange tapes, for 750m/10mins to the metalled Prodromos-Platres road at a green and white sign "Prodhromos Dam 6k". Turn right downhill for 50m and hairpin left down an earth road.

Ignore all forks to the right on a gradual descent round a steep, rocky and wooded mountainside. Look right for wide views across lowland villages to further ranges of hills. Reach a T-junction with another earth road.

[2.6kms/1½mls/40mins]

(Trooditissa Monastery is 1km up the hill to the left. Details in Olympus Walk 8.)

Turn right, downhill for 50m and take the next turning left, marked with a blue arrow on a rock. Look for red/white marker-tapes and descend a zig-zag track generally southward with views across Foini and farmland. To the left, the wooded hillside rises steeply. Ignore any uphill forks; at all other junctions, descend left. Reach Foini at two cafes and a metalled road. Walk downhill and bear left into Foini (alt. 900m/3000ft): war memorial, Co-op mini-market, taxi, cafes.

[4kms/2½mls/1¼hrs]

The number of faded blue Makarios signs on the walls shows the EOKA allegiance of Foini. Villagers make traditional furniture and chairs, lace and costume, carved wooden chests. Using local clay, pottery was the original industry of Foini. An enthusiast, Mr Pivlakis, has collected examples of traditional pots in a village house and yard.

From the Co-op, follow a street of old houses curving right to the Pivlakion Pottery Museum. Ascend left out of the far end of the village past a Taxi sign and follow the road sign "Limassol 48k" up a zig-zag road cutting for 400m. Above a concrete embankment on the left, a red arrow indicates a path rising south-east up a gully to join the metalled minor road F821. (Missing the red arrow doesn't matter. The minor road is to the left at the top of the cutting.) Ascend left to a T-junction. Platres is right, east, along Kalidonion Street past a board of hotel signs.

[3.5kms/2½mls/1hr]

TROODOS: WALK 2   Grade ** linear
Prodromos to Moutoullas via Pedoulas

This linear walk is marvellously varied, passing through forest and
farmland, visiting two little churches. On mule-trail, back roads and
cart-tracks, it wriggles round valleys and along ridges. The route
links three villages in the fertile Marathasa region of North Troodos.

Logistics
Start-point: Prodromos.
Total: 17.25kms/10¹/₂mls/5hrs, down 610m/2000ft.
Finish: Moutoullas, 9kms/5¹/₂mls by road from Prodromos.
                There's no taxi in Moutoullas. The safest arrangement
                may be to take car and taxi from Pedoulas or
                Prodromos down to Moutoullas, leave the car there
                and shuttle back in the taxi to the start-point. Taxis
                (1994) in Prodromos: tel. 462041; in Pedoulas: Katarina
                tel. 952414, or find the Rural Taxi at Luna Park corner,
                near the Mountain Rose restaurant.

2.1 Prodromos to Pedoulas
Start at the north-east end of Prodromos (alt. 1390m/4560ft) at a 5-
road junction with room to park. Opposite a supermarket and the
Prodromos Restaurant are a telephone kiosk, a water tap and a
shrine.

Walk north-north-west down a minor road signed to the Forestry
College. Pass WCs, post office. At the college entrance [300m], turn
right along the east side of a football pitch and then bend left for
20m.

Take an earth road hairpinning steeply down right for 15m
towards a white bollard. Fork left for 20m. Where the earth road
turns right again, continue straight ahead down a few metres and
go right on a sunken mule-trail. After 300m, avoid a gully dropping
down to the right: follow the trail up left, to curve counter-clockwise,
before descending a rough, sandy gully. Fork right and zig-zag
down past Bollard 596 to a concrete tank by the road to Pedoulas
(*ped-oo-lass*).
[2.5kms/1¹/₂mls/³/₄hr]

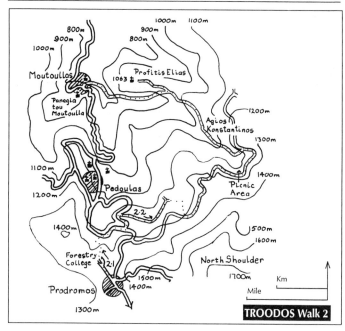

TROODOS Walk 2

Turn right and walk 1km along the road to the next left turn. Follow a Harry's Springwater Vrysi Restaurant sign down this side-road for 900m. Turn right for 300m to an hotel (alt. 1220m/4000ft). [2.25kms/1¹/₂mls/40mins]

2.2 Pedoulas to Moutoullas

Continue eastward past the hotel for 100m and fork left on an earth road. Look for yellow waymarks and orange tape-markers. Curve counter-clockwise round a re-entrant with a wooded and terraced valley below to the left. 1km/¹/₄hr from the hotel, ignore a red arrow pointing left at a T-junction: ascend right, east, on a woodland track to another T-junction at Pole 251. Ascend right, south, for 150m to a very wide earth road.
[1.75kms/1ml/¹/₂hr]

Turn left for 1.5kms/1ml/20mins to a shaded picnic area on the left, with a water-point (alt. 1300m/4265ft). Curve counter-clockwise

for another 900m/12mins to a green/white signpost "Pinewood 3½M, Stavroulia 1½M, Dead End Road". Follow the Dead End sign down left from the main earth road. (The wide earth road continues to Kakopetria.)
[2.5kms/1½mls/35mins]

Descend a rocky forest road, going right at all forks, for 2kms/ 1¼mls until cultivation starts - and shade stops - at Agios Konstantinos (alt. 1075m/3525ft). Fork left here down past concrete water tanks and a few buildings among vineyards and orchards.
[2.3kms/1½mls/½hr]

After the tanks, take right forks for 1km to an illegible blue metal sign on the right. This right-hand track goes up for 1.2kms to a little church, Profitis Elias, perched on a summit with views all round (alt. 1063m/3487ft).
[3.5kms/2¼mls/1hr]

Back on the main track, continue downhill, making right forks. The road levels out, with orchards filling the terraced valley below to the left. Across the valley, the village of Moutoullas comes into view to the west. Look down to see the way into the village: a concrete track winding over a stream-bed. After double power Pole KJ 13 above to the right, fork left down past Pole KJ 18-1 to the stream-bed.
[2kms/1¼mls/40mins]

Walk up the concrete road past a water-point and an octagonal chapel to Pole 99. (The local sweet, *soutjoukas*, is made a few steps further on, near the church.) Turn uphill at Pole 99 and emerge above Moutoullas (alt. 780m/2560ft) on the main road due south of the church by a shop "Mini Market EAΣH" and cafes.
[500m]

Opposite is a shrine and a sign to Panagia Tou Moutoulla church. To see this late Byzantine church, ask for the key at the cafe just uphill to the left, or the house below the church. Follow the church arrow up a minor metalled road, turning left at a water tank, up a mule-trail.
[500m]

Moutoullas claims its pears to be the best in Cyprus. Villagers carve traditional pinewood troughs still used across the island as mixing bowls or clothes tubs.

131

Village and church share the name of the family that built the church in 1279 and are included in a fresco there. The church is listed by the UN as a world heritage cultural treasure. It has a protective roof over its own timbers, carved doors, and frescos.

TROODOS: WALK 3
Grade ** circuit
Chandria - Madari Ridge - Mount Adhelfi circuit

Follow farmers' roads westward along a hillside, through orchards and vineyards, with views almost all the way. Rise gradually to cross the hill-top ridge into another valley. Take a Nature Trail eastward along the Madari ridge with views on both sides. Reach Mount Adhelfi, the island's second highest summit and then curve down a rough road to the starting point.

Walking is easy underfoot. There is occasional shade in the first section and more along the ridge. Look for orange tape-markers.

Logistics

Start-point: Chandria *(khan-dree-ah)* village (alt. 1190m/3900ft) is 18kms/11mls by road east of Troodos. It has shops and cafes. A big new white church with red roof stands at the east end of the village. Follow signs for "Lagoudera 7k; Saranti 8k" up the road beside the church. After 1km, just after two circular water tanks on the left, park opposite the next left turn, an earth road (alt. 1350m/4420ft).

Total: 13kms/8mls/4^{1}/2hrs, up and down 260m/850ft.

Finish: At start-point.

Chandria (alt. 1190m/3900ft) was founded by Genoese settlers in the 15th century. The pillars in the church are made from single pine trunks.

Ascend the earth road, hairpinning westward back from the metalled road. Fork left, downhill, parallel to the metalled road. Stay on the major track which becomes sandy as it contours west and then ascends across a hillside of vineyards. Fork left, counter-clockwise on to a clear sandy road with views to the left, across Chandria, a reservoir and Kyperounta village.

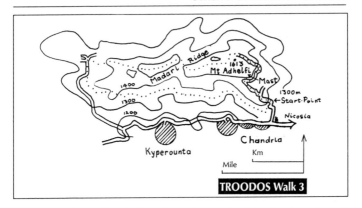

Fork right, still uphill on the major track: the asbestos mine at Pano Amiandos comes into view to the south-west. Go under power-lines at Pole KM 39-6, still ascending and then contouring, to a T-junction with Kyperounta below left.
[1.5kms/1ml/35mins]

Turn right, going north-west towards the skyline ridge. Stay on the contour, ignoring a left fork downhill, and walk counter-clockwise round a re-entrant to a slab of concrete buttressing. Turn up right, past some breeze-block huts (water tap), to a pole above a water tank on the skyline.
[1km/¹/₂ml/20mins]

Over this ridge, the landscape changes as vineyards are left behind. Pass Bollard 844 and fork up right to curve clockwise round two spurs. Ignore a hairpin fork up right and stay on the contour, curving clockwise through pine trees to emerge above cultivated valleys. Another big reservoir appears. Reach a crossroads among vineyards. Turn right for 400m to another wide track junction and Nature Trail shelter (alt. 1350m/4430ft).
[2.25kms/1¹/₂mls/40mins]

This is the Madari (*mad-arry*) Nature Trail. From the shelter, ascend right, south-eastward, up a stony track. The ridge rises eastward, mostly shaded by pines. Chandria and Kyperounta are again visible below. There are views left and right to the sea on the north and south coasts.

After 40mins the rest of the ridge opens up ahead, bare and

133

rocky, culminating in a peak-top hut. To reach Adhelfi *(add-elf-ee)* summit, turn right off the Nature Trail at a seat signed "Viewpoint" and ascend over rocks for a few minutes (alt. 1613m/5292ft). Resume the trail for 200m to its end on an open col.
[4kms/2¹/₂mls/1¹/₂hrs]

A path goes up to the peak-top hut, a fire look-out station with all-round views. Below it, a Nature Trail descends left for an extra 2.2kms/1¹/₂mls circuit of this peak.

Leave the col on a rough road descending south-east and curving clockwise down round the summit for 750m to a signals mast. Chandria comes into view. Stay on this road, now mostly with a metalled surface, for another ¹/₂hr to a road junction.

Follow the "Chandria 3k" arrow down to the right, with views of the first half of the walk. The Mount Olympus radar globe is ahead on the skyline. Curve clockwise down for 1km/20mins to the start-point.
[4.25kms/2¹/₂mls/1¹/₄hrs]

In Lagoudera village, 7kms/4¹/₂mls north of Chandria, Panagia tou Araka church is famous for its 12th century Byzantine paintings.

A self-guided Nature Trail [7kms/4¹/₂mls] is scheduled to start at the church.

TROODOS: WALK 4   Grade *** out-and-back/linear
Mount Papoutsa

At the eastern end of the Troodos range, Mount Papoutsa, third highest peak of Cyprus, reaches 1554m/5098ft. It's the same way up and down, much of it stony and rough. Keen winds can make the top ridge uncomfortable - and snow sprinkles the summit in winter.

After the descent, a pleasant walk leads down through farmland to Agros village. There is no water on the way.

Logistics

Start-point: The road junction 6.5kms/4mls south-west of Palaichori on the road to Agros. A road leads south-west signed "Agios Theodoros 3k". Agros is 8kms away by road.

Total: 10kms/6¼mls/3¾hrs, up 275m/900ft, down 555m/1820ft.

Finish: Either at the start-point, or at Agros, where there are taxis. The Agros bus runs to Limassol daily at 0700, returning at 1200: 75c. *(NB: Always check current transport details on the spot.)*

4.1 The summit

From the junction (alt. 1280m/4200ft), walk 50m down the Palaichori road, north-eastward, to a hairpin bend. Pick a way up to the right over a bulldozed bank of earth onto the end of a spur. This leads south-east and then south, before swinging eastward up to the summit, marked by a wooden cross above a hunters' stone shelter (alt. 1554m/5098ft).
[2kms/1¼mls/1hr]

A rocky ridge descends south-east from here for those who want an extension or further views. The track vanishes as it descends over loose stones into spiny scrub.

Return to the start-point by reversing the ascent. Aim for the hairpin bend on the road, which bends out of sight behind the spur. [2kms/1¼mls/40mins]

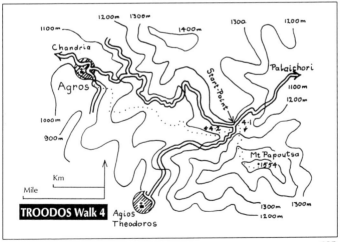

4.2 To Agros

For the walk down to Agros *(ag-ross)*, go back 25m to the road junction. Bisect the two roads and scramble down 500m through dumped rubbish to a broad earth road coming in from the left. Keep straight on, past a road hairpinning off to the left, keeping the valley on the left. The road ascends past a breeze-block building to the right, reaching a col.

Leave the road there and walk left for 25m. Turn right down a sunken mule-track between low stone walls. Emerge into a valley where the track contours round the hillside with vineyards below to the right. Take the first fork right down a similar track, past a concrete pond on the left and up to an earth road.

Turn left on this and follow it south-west with the valley on the left. Curve counter-clockwise round a re-entrant, ignoring the track up right at its head. The road curves right and Agros comes into view on the right, to the north. Head for a signals mast and hairpin right, down below it. Continue to the metalled road at the south end of Agros (alt. 1000m/3280ft).

Turn right and walk westward up into the village, following the Agros road sign at a road fork. Agros has cafes, shops, taxis, hotels, banks.

[6kms/3³/₄mls/2hrs]

Facing south from its hillside, Agros collects the sun and grows good grapes. Its water is pure enough to be bottled and sold. Monks from Asia Minor settled here in the 9th century.

✳   ✳   ✳